'Amy transforms the flat landscape of stories we think we kn___ ___ ___lly coloured stumpwork, full of unexpected detail, and ___ ___ t narrative – a Bayeux tapestry of the possib___ ___ denly seeing familiar images throuf'
Caroline Chartres, contributing ed.

'A masterpiece in metaphor. In *Image___ ___ ___ ___ ___ the door for us to understand abstract concepts in c___ ___ ___ ___, ushering us into the presence of God. With engaging anecdot___ ___ and a winsome exploration of the biblical stories, she proves a helpful guide to not only sin and atonement but also forgiveness and restoration. A book to return to again and again during Lent – I highly recommend it.'
Amy Boucher Pye, author of *7 Ways to Pray*

'*Images of Grace* did my soul much good. Amy does not simply teach us daily truths; she immerses us in daily experiences of the gospel. I found it very moving. Highly recommended.'
Glen Scrivener, author and evangelist at Speak Life

'Amy is a writer of rare talent. Here, she brings her rich theological insight and deep appreciation of metaphor to the topic of forgiveness. Ideally suited for Lent, read it for the fresh sense of wonder at God's mercy.'
Tanya Marlow, lecturer in pastoral theology, author of *Those Who Wait*

'*Images of Grace* invites us into a refreshing journey of restoration and transformation. With real-life illustrations and beautiful, lyrical writing, it is like a warm and soothing welcome into God's story of love over us, with fresh and enticing insights that take us to new places of intimacy and purpose with God. Well-known passages of scripture are explored in new ways that spark the imagination, with images that both assure and instruct.'
Liz Carter, author and poet

'As an oceanographer, having been in large storms at sea, I was particularly struck by, and found helpful and challenging, the meditations on Jonah.'
Professor Meric Srokosz, author of *Blue Planet, Blue God*

BRF

15 The Chambers, Vineyard
Abingdon OX14 3FE
brf.org.uk

Bible Reading Fellowship (BRF) is a charity (233280)
and company limited by guarantee (301324),
registered in England and Wales

ISBN 978 1 80039 117 8
First published 2022
10 9 8 7 6 5 4 3 2 1 0
All rights reserved

Text © Amy Scott Robinson 2022
This edition © Bible Reading Fellowship 2022
Cover illustrated by Ben Bloxham

The author asserts the moral right to be identified as the author of this work

Acknowledgements
Unless otherwise stated, scripture quotations are taken from The New Revised
Standard Version of the Bible, Anglicised edition, copyright © 1989, 1995 by the
Division of Christian Education of the National Council of the Churches of Christ in
the United States of America. Used by permission. All rights reserved.

Every effort has been made to trace and contact copyright owners for material
used in this resource. We apologise for any inadvertent omissions or errors, and
would ask those concerned to contact us so that full acknowledgement can be
made in the future.

A catalogue record for this book is available from the British Library

Printed and bound by CPI Group (UK) Ltd, Croydon CR0 4YY

Amy Scott Robinson

images *of* grace

*a journey from
darkness to light
at Easter*

BRF

for Cecily and Ilias
(with thanks for all the help with Greek)

Contents

Introduction

At the heart of the Christian message is a collection of abstract nouns. Love, sin, forgiveness, grace – it is difficult to explain the gospel message without using some or all of these words. The problem with abstract nouns is that, when we use them, we assume that the person we are talking to understands them. Not only that, we assume that they have the same understanding of the word that we do.

I first had the idea for this book because I didn't think that most of the people I talked to had a clear understanding of what sin and grace actually are. I often felt that I was meaning one thing by a word I used, while they were understanding another; and I was beginning to realise that my own definitions of these words were somewhat shaky.

The only way to understand huge abstract concepts, such as sin and forgiveness, is to look at images of them. For example, how would you explain to an alien being what love is? You might point them towards an example of two people in love, tell them a story or read them a poem. You might try to explain, in concrete terms, the behaviour that you would expect from somebody who loves you. All the time, you would be skirting around this big abstract concept of 'love', getting closer to defining and understanding it, testing out its shape and size from different angles. And if you kept going, your alien friend would have a better idea of what love is like. To know what it actually is, you would tell them, you have to experience it yourself; and even then, if you had to define it, you would only be adding your own images, stories and poems.

When it comes to defining God's grace, there are other abstract nouns packed away inside the first one. Grace has to do with forgiveness, and how can we understand forgiveness if we can't define sin, from which we are forgiven? In this book, we are going to take these abstractions one by one and discover how scripture describes them to us: namely, with images.

The Bible offers us a wide range of images for each of these concepts. It's important to have lots of metaphors and similes to describe abstract things, because no single one of them is exactly accurate. The more we have, the better the understanding that gets built up by all the different pictures. Some of the images are single similes: for example, sin is like turning away from God. Some of them are more extended metaphors: for example, sin is a stain, which means that forgiveness is like being cleaned. Some are whole stories: for example, the parable of the prodigal son, which offers metaphors for sin, repentance, forgiveness, acceptance and grace. We will explore all of those different kinds of images.

Lent is traditionally a time of repentance, fasting and prayer as we prepare to celebrate our salvation at Easter. This Lent, I hope that you will enjoy using this book to approach the concepts of repentance, sin, forgiveness and grace from some new angles, and arrive at Holy Week and Easter with a fresher, richer understanding of God's grace through the death and resurrection of Jesus.

I

Images of sin and repentance

Psalm 51 is said to have been written by King David after his disastrous affair with Bathsheba. The story, told in 2 Samuel 11–12, plays out like a Shakespearean tragedy: from the moment he sees and desires Bathsheba, David is dragged into deeper and deeper layers of sin and deceit. His attempts to cover the traces of his wrongdoing culminate in the murder of Bathsheba's husband, Uriah. Only when confronted by the prophet Nathan does David fully see and admit his sin. His repentance is poured out in a desperate prayer, which appears not in the book of 2 Samuel, but in the Psalms. In the text, Psalm 51 is attributed to David 'when the prophet Nathan came to him, after he had gone in to Bathsheba'.

While reading commentaries on Psalm 51, I was interested to learn that there are three Hebrew words used for sin, each given a different English translation in most versions: transgression, iniquity and sin. The words have different roots, and each of them is a little metaphor. The root of the word translated 'transgression' contains the image of rebelling, going in the opposite direction or against something. The root of the word translated 'iniquity' holds the idea of something bent or twisted out of shape. And the root of the word translated 'sin' means to miss, in the sense of a footballer hitting the goalpost or an arrow flying wide of the target. All three words appear in the first two verses of the psalm and continue to be used interchangeably throughout.

I am not a Hebrew scholar, so I feel cautious about making a big point out of these three descriptions. After all, in English, as in any language, we generally use words without thinking very deeply about their etymological roots; that's just how language develops. But it's worth noting that even these ancient words for sin come from attempts to explain and describe what sin is. These tiny word-based metaphors are a great example of our grappling with a concept that sits slightly beyond human understanding.

As ever with such concepts, having more than one image or metaphor to consider is useful: it helps us not to try to pin down, or box in, ideas that are larger than our human experience. David, in this psalm, uses several different poetic images for sin that go far beyond these simple words, and as we begin our exploration of God's forgiveness, it will be helpful for us to look at these. Alongside David, we can discover what it means to have sinned, what that experience is like and why it is important in terms of our relationship with God.

Our exploration of Psalm 51 will take us from Ash Wednesday, the first day of Lent, through to the end of the week. Then, from Sunday onwards, we will look at some other scriptural images of repentance, in the stories of Jonah and the prodigal son.

Ash Wednesday

David: sin is
a stain that needs cleaning

Have mercy on me, O God,
    according to your steadfast love;
according to your abundant mercy
    blot out my transgressions.
Wash me thoroughly from my iniquity,
    and cleanse me from my sin...
Purge me with hyssop, and I shall be clean;
    wash me, and I shall be whiter than snow.
PSALM 51:1–2, 7

In the introduction to this section, I mentioned how even the etymology of certain words can contain metaphors. One example of this is the word 'impeccable', which has come to mean something like 'spotless' in modern use. It comes from Latin words meaning 'without sin'. So there, hiding away in everyday use, is the notion that sin is like a dirty stain, and that to be without it is to be clean.

The last time I bought a car, the salesman tried to persuade me to pay quite a bit of extra money to have the upholstery treated with a stain-repellent formula. Apparently this magical stuff not only made the seats easier to clean, but also, by some miracle of chemistry, stopped them from getting dirty in the first place. Sensing my scepticism, he went on to regale me with tales of every time his own car had been in danger of destruction but had escaped spotless, including a particularly graphic description of picking up his daughter and her inebriated friends from what had clearly been an eventful and possibly illegal party. Nonetheless, I decided against buying the product and returned to my old car with its trodden-in crumbs, toddler handprints and inexplicable red wax melted into one of the seats. I was certain that even the chemical experts would have been defeated by my family's extraordinary talent for mess.

Unlike my salesman's upholstery, the human soul is not good at repelling the stain of sin. In fact, more like my own car, we seem to be attracted to it. Once sin lands on us, it clings and spreads. It melts into the seats like red wax. It stains like beetroot juice on a white tablecloth.

This had been exactly David's experience. For a start, he had left himself open to temptation: staying at home instead of accompanying his soldiers into battle, he was wandering around the roof of his palace, restless, at a loose end. When he saw Bathsheba bathing on her own roof, he could not resist finding out about her. I wonder whether he told himself, at first, that this was as far as it would go – merely satisfying his idle curiosity? But once he knew who she was, he had to meet her; having brought her to the palace, he slept with her, presumably against her will; once he knew she was pregnant, he embarked on a campaign of deceit to cover his tracks, which ended in the murder of her husband. In fact, David was making his way steadily through the ten commandments and breaking the lot: envying another man's wife, stealing, adultery, bearing false witness, murder.

David, having spent a long time trying to cover and hide his sin, realised that in God's eyes it was, and always had been, like a stain: obvious and shameful. Have you ever seen one of those daytime television programmes where experts go in with swabs and UV lights to discover how filthy the hotel room *really* is? In the same way, though David might have thought he'd succeeded in hiding his sin from other people, he had forgotten that it would always be visible to God.

Nathan the prophet had the same effect as the person who comes in to show the horrified hotel owner or hapless family the results from the lab: the exact levels of contamination, the health risks, all the previously invisible stains lit up blue. And the longer you leave a stain, the harder it is to get out. David's sin was indelible. Lives had been taken and destroyed, a family ripped apart, marriage vows broken and forcibly made. Yet his immediate reaction to Nathan was: 'I have sinned against the Lord' (2 Samuel 12:13). He knew that, for all the people he had hurt, it was God who saw the stain and only God who could clean it.

The many verbs David uses in these verses of Psalm 51 pour out in a desperate plea: blot out, wash me, cleanse me, purge me! Once we become aware of a mark on a piece of clothing, suddenly we notice it all the time and imagine that everyone else does too. Our eyes are drawn constantly towards the stain. In the same way, now that David has been presented with the truth about his sin, he desperately and urgently wants to get rid of it. This is not something that David is able to sort out for himself: he brings it to God to be cleaned thoroughly, 'whiter than snow'. There were bleaching techniques in ancient Israel, but the idea of cloth becoming 'whiter than snow' would have been a bold exaggeration in David's day, an image that underlines how only God would be able to achieve the kind of impossible spotlessness required.

In verse 7, David mentions a plant called hyssop, not because it was used in soap but because it was part of symbolic spiritual cleansing. It was hyssop that was used to sprinkle sacrificial blood in temple rituals and to paint the blood of the Passover lambs on to the door frames when God rescued his people from Egypt. With this image, David asks God to clean his soul, the 'inward being' and 'secret heart' that he mentioned in verse 6. This, too, acknowledges the depth of what he has done. He is drawing on the imagery of blood, sacrifice, ritual and prayer to wash away this sin. He sees God in the role of the temple priest, sprinkling with the hyssop to purify him.

I wonder whether we have anything like this reaction when we know that we have done wrong in the eyes of God. Even if our sin is not as catastrophic as David's, are we as anxious to rid ourselves of the stain?

It's true that for Christians, because of Jesus, we know that we are forgiven, loved and accepted. The sacrificial blood David pleads for comes from the cross. All the same, if we become complacent or neglectful about some of the stains that have soaked in, we risk forgetting how momentous that really is.

On the other hand, there are some stains that we prefer to cover up, rather than offering them to God to be cleaned. There are some things that feel too terrible, too impossible to imagine they could ever be forgiven. That's when it's good to remember that God is not a used-car salesman. He really can deliver on his promise to make us as spotless as snow.

A question

What protects a heart from being stained by sin?

A prayer

Lord, thank you for blotting out my transgressions. Wash me thoroughly, cleanse me, purge me. If you wash me, I really will be clean. Amen

Thursday

David: sin is brokenness and misery

Let me hear joy and gladness;
  let the bones that you have crushed rejoice...
Restore to me the joy of your salvation,
  and sustain in me a willing spirit...
The sacrifice acceptable to God is a broken spirit;
  a broken and contrite heart, O God, you will not despise.
PSALM 51:8, 12, 17

'Let me see some tenderness connected with a death,' said Scrooge, 'or that dark chamber, Spirit, which we left just now, will be forever present to me.' This is the moment in Charles Dickens' *A Christmas Carol* when Ebenezer Scrooge has reached the turning point of his famous journey from grumpy old miser to generous lover of Christmas. The third and final spirit has shown Scrooge reactions to his own death, which has caused nothing but relief for his debtors and the chance for his housemaid to steal his best shirt and bed curtains. Agonised by this consequence of his life of avarice and cruelty, Scrooge begs for a vision of some tenderness connected with a death, any death, to relieve the horror of the vision of his own lonely demise.

That passage came to mind as I read David's words in verse 8: 'Let me hear joy and gladness.' It's the cry of a person in a place so dark that all hints of relief from the relentless despair have been filtered out. The effect of being confronted with his sin has plunged David into misery, and he begs for a moment of light. Just like Scrooge, David finds his own actions and their consequences full of horrors.

Nathan the prophet was very clever when God sent him to David. He didn't go straight into making the accusation, putting the king on the defensive. Instead, he told a story about a rich man stealing a beloved lamb from his poor neighbour and killing it to eat (2 Samuel 12:1–4). David was furious with the thief, saying that he deserved to die and that he must pay back what he had taken, at which point Nathan finally spoke the words that pierced through to David's heart: 'You are the man!' (2 Samuel 12:7). David was caught out by metaphor. Perhaps, as the poet who wrote so many psalms, he should have seen it coming; but he didn't. Scrooge, David and the rest of us can be surprisingly deluded when it comes to our own wrongdoings, until a spiritual guide points it out.

By letting David judge the severity of the wrongdoing before accusing him of it, Nathan allowed him to see what he had done through the eyes of a powerful judge; in other words, he saw what it all looked like from God's perspective. I wonder whether that's why David writes, 'Let the bones that you have crushed rejoice.' He felt that moment of conviction like a crushing weight, suddenly trapping and flattening him. Sin might feel light while we're in it, but when we see it through God's eyes, it becomes too heavy for us to lift.

For David, sin is heavy, dark and miserable. It has become something from which he needs rescue: 'Restore to me the joy of your salvation,' he writes, aware that he has lost not only his joy, but also his confidence that God is going to help and save him.

In the end, though, for both David and Ebenezer Scrooge, the darkest moment is the only way into the light. The heaviness of sin may be crushing, but our awareness of how trapped we are in it can lead us to call out for help to the only one able to lift the weight. David knew this, too: he wrote that God would not despise a broken spirit and heart. Sin breaks the spirit, but a broken spirit leads us back to God.

A question

Who, or what, are your spiritual guides? How would you react if some-one pointed out your sin?

A prayer

Lord, some of the consequences of sin in this world make me feel crushed. When I come close to despair, may I call your name through the darkness. Thank you for offering welcome and rescue to broken hearts and crushed spirits. Amen

David: sin is separation from God

Hide your face from my sins,
    and blot out all my iniquities…
Do not cast me away from your presence,
    and do not take your holy spirit from me.

PSALM 51:9, 11

In a late 19th-century painting by Emil Keyser, two children have been caught scrumping. An old woman with a broom points an outstretched finger at them as they move sullenly into the foreground of the painting. The boy, ears red with shame, hangs his head and shoves his hands into his pockets. The girl, still clutching an apple, hunches her shoulders and seems to be listening to the old woman over her shoulder. The painting is titled *Explusion from the Garden of Eden*.

It's an original take on a much-depicted biblical scene. The very first disobedience of humankind resulted in being sent away from the presence of God and from a paradise; and the next thing to happen in the book of Genesis is another sin and a further distance, with Adam's son Cain moving 'away from the presence of the Lord' after murdering his brother (Genesis 4:16). Perhaps this is not a metaphor for sin so much as a direct consequence of it. If you steal apples, you will be sent out of the orchard.

But David knew there was more to it than that. All his life, he had enjoyed a close relationship with God. The evidence is there in all the other psalms he wrote as well as this one, not least his most famous work, Psalm 23, about God his shepherd being with him even in the darkest valley, his presence a comfort. 'Surely goodness and mercy shall follow me all the days of my life,' he wrote (v. 6). He had so much to lose.

As David listened to Nathan speaking God's words, he must have been cut to the heart, not because they were the words of an angry God, but because they were the words of a hurt and puzzled friend. You can read them for yourself in 2 Samuel 12:7–9. God lists all the things he has done for David, adding that if they had not been enough, more would have been added; and then he asks why David has despised him. God's first words to David, before moving on to the consequences of this sin, make it clear that a relationship has been broken.

Sin itself can be seen as separation. It's the first step in the wrong direction; a movement, however small, along a path that sends us away from God. So David asks God to hide his face from his sins, knowing that the relationship cannot persist while God looks at the things he has done. Then he begs not to be cast away from God's presence; he asks to be allowed to keep God's spirit. Perhaps he was thinking of his predecessor, Saul, who had lost that precious presence. Today, through Jesus, we know that we have the Holy Spirit in and among us always; David had only the memory of a once-favoured king losing everything. The fear of losing that guiding presence he had known all his life was very real.

There's something about the old woman in Emil Keyser's painting. Her face is not angry, and she isn't shouting or shaking a fist. She looks, if anything, tired; she's looking down, rather than towards the two children. The broom she is holding could have been used for beating the children, but instead she is leaning on it. Even the hand with the pointing finger droops a little. She looks almost as sorry as the two children that they have to go away.

David, fully aware of all the people he had wronged, knew that he had damaged his relationship with God and was on his way out of God's loving presence. The most important thing for him was to find his way back, not to a God who was banishing him, but to a friend he had abandoned.

A question

When have you felt separated from a friend or family member? What caused the separation, and did (or could) anything restore it?

A prayer

Father, help me to value my relationship with you as highly as David did. When I take steps away from you, turn me around quickly and show me the way back. Amen

David: sin damages the heart

You desire truth in the inward being;
   therefore teach me wisdom in my secret heart…
Create in me a clean heart, O God,
   and put a new and right spirit within me.
PSALM 51:6, 10

I am very fond of the BBC television show *The Repair Shop*. Perhaps you think I'm a bit soft, but to me there is something Jesus-like in all those stories of restoration, all those sentimental items brought back to life, and I rarely make it through an episode dry-eyed. One of my favourite examples was the man who brought in a reel-to-reel tape player from 1962, complete with several tapes of himself as a boy, singing with his father at the piano. The player had developed a fault: instead of playing back the tapes, it had started to wipe them. The owner didn't dare to fiddle with the machine himself, in case he caused further damage. Worried that he would lose the only remaining recording of his father singing, he had stopped trying to play the tapes at all.

Repairing the reel-to-reel recorder was an intricate job. Various bits of the electrical components had to be replaced altogether with modern alternatives, as did the worn drive belt in the heart of the machine. Then everything was cleaned of years of accumulated dirt. The team restored the player to its owner, who listened with tears in his eyes to his own voice as a little boy, blending with the deeper voice of his father.

In these verses of Psalm 51, David asks God to create a clean heart in him. It's a phrase that echoes back to the beginning of his story.

The prophet Samuel had warned Israel against appointing a king in the first place, and his patience quickly wore thin with Saul. Early in Saul's reign, Samuel asked the king to wait for seven days for him to come and offer the sacrifices required to go into battle against the Philistines. Saul, following the letter of the law, barely held on until the week was up before panicking and offering the sacrifice himself. Samuel arrived before the smoke had stopped rising and made it clear that already Saul was on his way out. 'The Lord has sought out a man after his own heart,' he told the king (1 Samuel 13:14). That was who Saul was supposed to be: a man after God's own heart. Someone who would follow the intention, and not the letter. Someone who would deeply understand the aims and purposes of the Lord, not panic and pay lip service to the prophet's instructions while thinking he knew better.

Much later, when God told Samuel to go and anoint a new king from among Jesse's sons, he reminded him: 'Do not look on his appearance… for the Lord does not see as mortals see; they look on the outward appearance, but the Lord looks on the heart' (1 Samuel 16:7). Saul had been the tallest of his tribe, literally head and shoulders above the rest – that might even be where we get the phrase from (1 Samuel 10:23). David was the youngest of eight brothers, overlooked while he watched over the sheep. But God was looking for a man after his own heart, and he chose David.

I wonder whether David's mind wandered over any of that when, writing Psalm 51, he asked God to teach him wisdom in his secret heart. Just as God had seen David's heart all those years ago, David knew that God could see it now, and he knew that it was not in a good state. It needed to be filled with the words of God's wisdom instead of the words of his own desires.

Phrases from the social media age, such as 'Follow your heart' and 'The heart wants what it wants', depict the heart as a force in its own right: whimsical, uncontrollable, inexplicable but ultimately correct. It's as if the heart's passions cannot be avoided, and to deny the heart would be to miss out on some sort of ultimate personal destiny. That's not how David would have seen it. He had just experienced the trouble caused by following the whims of his heart and probably would have agreed with Jeremiah, who called the heart 'devious above all else' (Jeremiah 17:9). His inward being was no longer telling him the truth that God desires, but had tricked him and led him outside God's will.

The fact that God chose David as a man after his own heart shows that it is possible to have a heart deeply rooted in God, rather than a wayward and fanciful one. But David knew that his once-faithful heart had been infected by sin and was in need of a cure. And not just a quick fix, either, but a re-creation of what had been there before. 'Create in me a clean heart, O God,' he wrote (v. 10).

The truth is that sin causes damage to our hearts. Like a drive belt in an old tape recorder, too much pulling in the wrong direction and snagging on things can force a heart out of shape and wear it thin, eventually leading it to do the opposite of what it was made to do. Trying to fix it ourselves can make things worse. Only the expert hands of a maker can clean it, and some parts may need re-creating and replacing altogether. But when we entrust our hearts into the hands of God, they will be restored and we will once again be able to hear, loud and clear, the sound of our Father's voice.

A question

What do you hear from your heart?

A prayer

God, I bring my heart to you. Examine it, and show me the parts that are out of shape. Create a clean heart in me, God, so that your voice and your wisdom are in the very centre of my being. Amen

David: wholehearted offering

O Lord, open my lips,
    and my mouth will declare your praise.
For you have no delight in sacrifice;
    if I were to give a burnt-offering, you would not be pleased.
The sacrifice acceptable to God is a broken spirit;
    a broken and contrite heart, O God, you will not despise.

PSALM 51:15–17

Acting as peacemaker in sibling arguments comes with the territory of having more than one child. I'm sure I'm not the only mother who has pulled apart two squealing children, with accusations (and small missiles) still being flung between them, and after a hopeless few minutes trying to get to the bottom of who started it, has barked: 'Just say sorry to each other and STOP!' I'm sure, also, that I'm not the only parent who has received every kind of apology except a real one: the pouting sorry, the shouted sorry, the door-slam sorry, and of course that sibling favourite: 'I'm sorry that *he's* so annoying!'

At one point, searching parenting websites for tips and reassurance, I came across what became known in our family as a 'proper sorry'. It involves four steps: name what you've done wrong; explain why it was wrong and how it hurt the other person; apologise; and say what you can do to make sure it doesn't happen again.

I would love to say that it worked like a charm, but there are no charms in parenting. It did, however, lead me to reflect on how I apologise as an adult, and how often my 'sorry' has been performative, acted out to keep the peace while deep down I remain convinced that I'm in the right.

The thing about a 'proper sorry' is that it can't be said quickly in the heat of the moment, so that the adult will leave you alone and you can get straight back to teasing your sister. It can't be said grumpily or gracelessly; there's simply too much of it to get through. It can't be said while you're still accusing the other person. And it can't even be convincingly acted. It takes time, reflection and distance from the event to manage it.

In other words, it's impossible to say a 'proper sorry' unless you really are sorry, which means that it is not the kind of apology a parent can insist on. It is precious and rare, both between our children and in any human relationship. I've taken to listening for the four steps whenever somebody in the news makes a public apology. They are very rarely all included.

In Psalm 51, David was anxious not just to go through the steps of repentance for show. As the king, he knew what words and actions would have satisfied the people around him, and he knew the sacrifices and rituals that a priest would be likely to ask him to undertake. But he sensed that God would not be pleased with the standard burnt offering. As we saw yesterday, the only way for David to repent was to hand over everything that his sin had broken, including himself, to God.

David begins these verses with 'Lord, open my lips.' It's as if he is aware that even opening his mouth of his own accord will lead him to stumble; he's handing over his speech to God in complete submission.

In verse 17, David recognises that repentance is a sacrifice. This is true even in human relationships. To truly apologise, we have to give something up. For a start, we are giving up our view of ourselves as in the right, which is very hard to part with. We lay aside all hope of justifying or excusing our actions. We also, in a sense, hand ourselves over to the other person: once we have acknowledged that we were wrong, we are letting them decide to accept the apology or to turn away. We face up to the possibility of a consequence for our actions.

In the same way, David says, his broken and contrite heart is a sacrifice to God. It's not transactional, like the burnt offering would be: specific offerings for specific sins. It's not given with an expectation that everything can then go straight back to normal. It's simply a handing over of the whole sorry mess. And David writes that God will not despise it. God knows a proper sorry when he hears one.

A question

How does it feel to receive an authentic, heartfelt apology?

A prayer

O Lord, open my lips, and my mouth will declare your praise. Lead my words, my actions and my thoughts in your ways: I give myself to you completely. Amen

Jonah: the sea

The sailors said to one another, 'Come, let us cast lots, so that we may know on whose account this calamity has come upon us.' So they cast lots, and the lot fell on Jonah. Then they said to him, 'Tell us why this calamity has come upon us. What is your occupation? Where do you come from? What is your country? And of what people are you?' 'I am a Hebrew,' he replied. 'I worship the Lord, the God of heaven, who made the sea and the dry land.' Then the men were even more afraid, and said to him, 'What is this that you have done!' For the men knew that he was fleeing from the presence of the Lord, because he had told them so.

Then they said to him, 'What shall we do to you, that the sea may quieten down for us?' For the sea was growing more and more tempestuous. He said to them, 'Pick me up and throw me into the sea; then the sea will quieten down for you; for I know it is because of me that this great storm has come upon you.'
JONAH 1:7–12

We are going to spend the next few days in the book of Jonah. You might like to get your Bible and read through the whole thing. It isn't long, and it's one of those Bible stories that can sometimes hold surprises simply because the versions we know from childhood have crowded out the actual text.

Jonah is a story about sin, repentance and the unchanging, predictable nature of God's mercy. It is full of rich metaphors for those things. I should mention from the start that, just because I am speaking of metaphors, this does not necessarily mean that I'm approaching the whole book as a metaphor or parable. It's presented in the Bible as history; but whichever way we read it, its images can hold the same meanings.

The story opens with God's direct instruction to Jonah to go and preach to Nineveh, which is a 'great city' full of 'wickedness' (Jonah 1:2). Early listeners to the story would only have needed the name 'Nineveh' to understand that these people were the worst of the worst. They were notorious for their cruelty in war and their merciless treatment of their captives. Speaking out against them would have been terrifying, but as we shall see later, fear was not the reason Jonah gave for his refusal to follow God's instruction.

To avoid the task, Jonah attempted to flee God's presence by getting on a boat bound for Tarshish, which may have been a real place at the time or may be shorthand for 'as far away as he could possibly get'. God responded with a mighty storm which threatened to break up the ship, and the sailors started to throw their cargo overboard, attempting to lighten the boat. Jonah, however, had gone below deck and was fast asleep. The sailors cast lots to find out which of them the storm was meant for, and when the lot fell on Jonah, they woke him up and started quizzing him.

Jonah had never been anything but honest with the sailors. Apparently he had already told them that he was fleeing from the presence of God (v. 10), but it was only when he gave them some specifics about *which* God he was trying to avoid that they became anxious. Describing God as the one 'who made the sea and the dry land' (v. 9) didn't leave much wiggle room for the idea that the ship might eventually escape God's territory.

Jonah, however, was remarkably calm, all things considered. Seeing that his actions had endangered the lives of other people, he knew at once that the only way the ship could be saved would be if he wasn't on it. His short speech to the sailors was grounded in logic.

Jonah had not yet reached a point of full repentance in his attitude, but his actions represent the beginning of that journey. By asking to be thrown into the sea, Jonah was physically and forcibly removing himself from the thing that was taking him away from God's plan and God's path. He was removing himself from the others who were at risk of being harmed by his sin as well. Unlike David before Nathan showed up, Jonah was perfectly self-aware: he knew exactly what he had tried to do and, seeing the consequences of it, he was prepared to undo it immediately, even if that meant sacrificing his life.

I said earlier that one theme in the story of Jonah is God's unchanging, predictable mercy. Jonah was absolutely clear and certain about the cause of the storm and its solution, but he also knew that to be thrown into the sea was to be thrown back on to the mercy of God. His prayer, which we will look at tomorrow, gives some hints of that.

Jonah's clear-eyed attitude to his own sin led him to take emergency evasive action which we can learn from when we feel we are heading in the wrong direction. What waves have we already caused with our actions? Who stands at risk of being harmed or caught up in our choices? What is carrying us away from God's plan, and is it possible, even at great risk, to get clear of it? As we shall see, it's better to be in the sea with God than in a boat without him.

A question

Do you need to jump ship?

A prayer

Dear God, some situations are just as terrifying to get out of as they are to stay in. Give me the courage to make the right choice. Help me to trust that there is safety in your will, O maker of the sea. Amen

Jonah: the belly of the fish

Then Jonah prayed to the Lord his God from the belly of the fish, saying,

'I called to the Lord out of my distress,
    and he answered me;
out of the belly of Sheol I cried,
    and you heard my voice…
The waters closed in over me;
    the deep surrounded me;
weeds were wrapped around my head
    at the roots of the mountains.
I went down to the land
    whose bars closed upon me forever;
yet you brought up my life from the Pit,
    O Lord my God.'

JONAH 2:1–2, 5–6

I have a confession. In all my time performing as a children's story-teller, I have told the story of Jonah countless times, in many different ways, including in rhyme, in song and with accompanying actions and whale vomit sound effects. But I have never got this part of the story quite correct. Jonah's prayer from the belly of the whale has been a blind spot for me, one of those oversights that can come from a story being so familiar from so early in childhood that it becomes part of the wallpaper of your brain. I repent, and I will try to set things right.

The problem is that in children's versions, the simplified story tends to be told something like this: 'Jonah didn't like it in the big fish. It was dark and smelly. He felt sorry. He prayed and asked for God's help. God answered his prayer and the big fish sicked Jonah up on the beach.' This gives the impression that the fish was a punishment and that Jonah, at his lowest point, prayed a prayer of repentance which resulted in his rescue – absolutely none of which appears in the text.

For a start, Jonah is far from experiencing the fish as the rock bottom of his experience up to this point. Instead, he vividly describes the experience of drowning, sinking to the bottom of the sea and being wrapped in weeds 'at the roots of the mountains' (v. 6). That was his moment of losing all hope, of thinking that he was going to die: 'The land whose bars closed upon me forever' (v. 6). He likens it to Sheol and the Pit, both names for the place of the dead. Then, when he says that God brought up his life from the Pit, he uses the past tense; it is not a hopeful future plea. God has already rescued him. The fish was not a punishment; the fish was the instrument of salvation for Jonah.

Second, there is still no hint of a repentant attitude in Jonah's prayer. There are no requests for forgiveness or acknowledgements of wrong-doing, neither is there any plea for help or rescue. Instead, the prayer is mainly one of praise and thanksgiving. Jonah recalls a previous prayer, made from the bottom of the sea: 'As my life was ebbing away,' he says, 'I remembered the Lord' (v. 7). And he is grateful that his call was heard and answered. Jonah finishes his prayer with a renewed promise of loyalty to God, but he compares himself with 'those who worship vain idols' (v. 8) and makes no mention of those who 'flee to Tarshish,' as he has actually done. The final line of the prayer sums it up: 'Deliverance belongs to the Lord!' (v. 9).

The way back to God from the consequences of sin may not be quick or easy. Sometimes placing ourselves back into God's will can feel like drowning or like sitting in the dark for three days. But with the attitude of Jonah, every step back towards God is taken along a path of thanks, in the knowledge that God is merciful and that we are already in the process of being saved.

Jonah's faith in God's mercy from the very moment of repentance is exactly the reason he gives later in the story for not wanting to preach to Nineveh. Jonah was all too aware of God's enormous capacity for grace, mercy and forgiveness, and he didn't want it to be extended to the worst people on earth. Every bit of the book of Jonah rings with that mercy because, as we discover by the end, it's the whole point of the story.

A question

Is there any sin outside of God's loving mercy?

A prayer

Lord, I want to take the very first step along a road that leads back to you. Thank you that you are already rescuing me. Salvation belongs to the Lord. Amen

Jonah: sackcloth and ashes

When the news reached the king of Nineveh, he rose from his throne, removed his robe, covered himself with sackcloth, and sat in ashes. Then he had a proclamation made in Nineveh: 'By the decree of the king and his nobles: No human being or animal, no herd or flock, shall taste anything. They shall not feed, nor shall they drink water. Human beings and animals shall be covered with sackcloth, and they shall cry mightily to God. All shall turn from their evil ways and from the violence that is in their hands. Who knows? God may relent and change his mind; he may turn from his fierce anger, so that we do not perish.'

JONAH 3:6–9

After an avalanche killed and injured many of its citizens, Austria declared a national day of mourning for the victims. An Austrian school friend of mine fashioned a black armband out of a sock and wore it to school, and I remember being impressed by the obvious patriotism that prompted such an outward display of his dedication to his homeland and identification with his people, even at a distance. Ours was a very international school, and people were often proud to note and celebrate events and special days from their own countries and cultures. But it would be very strange, in the 21st century, for a nation to require an outward show of mourning, let alone repentance, from every one of its citizens.

Over the past few years, we have seen many examples of whole organisations being called to account for their actions. Television companies, film studios, publishers and churches have been among the groups required to publicly apologise for the harmful cultures and abuses they have allowed to remain hidden for too long. Often, when the apology is made, it leaves in its wake a large number of employees and people on the fringes of the organisation, either making their own individual apologies or scrambling to distance themselves from all knowledge of whatever went on. In a society focused on individual culpability, we don't really have a working system to absolve a whole group of people at once.

In the Bible, there is precedent for a king or a prophet to repent on behalf of their people. Ezra did so with mourning and fasting (Ezra 10) and Daniel with sackcloth and ashes (Daniel 9:3–5). These physical signs of humility, grief and prayer were powerful symbols to these leaders' people that their collective wrongdoing needed to be addressed. Their actions also showed the people that prayers of repentance were being said for and about them. For the king of Nineveh, however, it was not enough to swap royal robes for sackcloth and to fast and pray himself. He required that everybody in Nineveh – and not only the human beings, but the animals too – should join in. Jonah's message hit home with such force that it prompted an immediate city-wide U-turn from evil and violence to sackcloth, ashes, fasting and loud wailing.

We have a little bit of the ancient symbolism of repentance left to us in Lent, when we might fast from certain foods or activities and, on Ash Wednesday, receive a little ash on our heads. For us today, it's a sign of humility before God, a remembrance that we are dust (mortal) and that we need constantly to realign ourselves with our Saviour. Like the ash in Nineveh, it is a collective symbol that reflects the sinful state of all humanity: it rolls the whole experience of being human and flawed and mortal into one. For me, it brings about deep and helpful reflection on those things.

However, I don't think that the precise symbolism of the sackcloth and ashes is the most important thing to take away from this part of the book of Jonah. Rather, I think it's the mention of those poor animals joining in.

Have you noticed that Jonah is a tale of exaggeration? Let's have a look at it so far:

- God told Jonah to go to the worst people on earth.
- Jonah ran away to the furthest imaginable place.
- A storm blew up that threatened to kill everybody.
- Jonah offered himself to be thrown into the sea.
- He was brought to shore by a gargantuan fish.
- He preached total destruction to the city of Nineveh.
- They were immediately so repentant that they even put sackcloth on the cows.

I hope I will be forgiven for suggesting that the writer of Jonah did not intend the account to be read entirely straight-faced. Everything is slightly cartoonish and larger than life, and it all leads towards the book's conclusion: that God is absurdly, ridiculously, hilariously and hugely merciful. In the book of Jonah, God's love and compassion know no bounds – and, of course, that is not an exaggeration at all. It's the humorous, exaggerated storytelling of the rest of the tale that brings us face to face with the truth: God is gracious well beyond our expectation or understanding.

A question

What do you think of the idea of collective repentance? Can a large group of people show remorse or be forgiven together?

A prayer

Lord, you are so gracious and compassionate that, at the first hint of repentance, you will forgive even him. And even her. And even them. And even me. Thank you. Amen

Thursday
_____

Jonah: the plant

The Lord God appointed a bush, and made it come up over Jonah, to give shade over his head… But when dawn came up the next day, God appointed a worm that attacked the bush, so that it withered… the sun beat down on the head of Jonah so that he was faint and asked that he might die. He said, 'It is better for me to die than to live'…

Then the Lord said, 'You are concerned about the bush, for which you did not labour and which you did not grow… And should I not be concerned about Nineveh, that great city, in which there are more than a hundred and twenty thousand people who do not know their right hand from their left, and also many animals?'

JONAH 4:6–11

I'm sure I'm not alone in my struggles with basic technology. Luckily, I live with someone who has the magic touch with computers. Often, I will try and fail for half an hour to do something, and then my husband will wander past and manage it in under five seconds – and, mystifyingly, I'm sure he is always doing something I've already tried. When he's not around to help, though, I do have a tendency to take out my frustrations on the machine itself. I know it can't hear me, but that only makes it all the more irritating. I remember once, after repeated refusals from my printer to actually print a document, squaring up to it and shouting: 'But… but you have ONE JOB!'

That's how Jonah felt about the plant which had grown up above his head. It was a thing, a weed, inconsequential really, except that it was doing one job: keeping him out of the sun. When it stopped fulfilling its intended purpose, he became irrationally angry about it.

I have long been slightly baffled by the ending of Jonah, because God seems to be comparing his compassion for Nineveh to the plant, for which Jonah felt no emotional attachment whatsoever; but this is probably another hangover from childhood retellings. Now I wonder whether the comparison has more to do with purpose. The plant's purpose, the only reason God made it grow at all, was to shade Jonah's head, and the worm made it fail in its purpose, so that the plant became both useless and dead. Human beings, on the other hand, were created with God at the very centre of their purpose. We were created out of God's love for us, to be in perfect relationship with our maker and with each other. Sin, like the worm, makes us fail in our purpose. The great city of Nineveh held more than 120,000 persons who, like the plant, would wither because they did not 'know their right hand from their left' (v. 11). They had no idea of the possibilities of joy and fulfilment that come with the knowledge of the living God, the reason for being human. So God asked Jonah to compare his concern for the plant's failure to do its one job to God's concern for all humanity missing out on their one spiritual purpose: to receive God's infinite love.

When I say that relationship with God is at the centre of our purpose, I don't mean that it's our function, as if God's reason for making humans was that he needed us to worship him. Rather, he designed us for relationship with him in the same way that a car might be designed to run on diesel rather than petrol. When you put the wrong fuel in the engine, it not only stops the vehicle from working properly, but also does damage which needs to be fixed before the correct fuel can be used again.

Jonah had been thinking of the people of Nineveh in terms of the *extent* of their sin: their violence, war crimes, torture and idolatry. To him, these things should have been unforgiveable and deserving of punishment. He hoped to see the city destroyed. The lesson of the plant was that God wasn't looking at the specific wrongdoings so much as the root of it all, the worm at the heart of it. To God, the city was already destroyed, already withered, because their essential relationship with God was missing. They had been using the wrong fuel all along. No wonder so much damage had been done.

The book finishes with this lesson, but we don't see Jonah's reaction at all. Perhaps this is to invite us to identify ourselves with Jonah's opinion, and to consider whether we have anything to learn from the lesson, not just of the plant but of what happened to Jonah and to Nineveh. Interestingly, in Jonah himself we never get an example of a repentant attitude. We never see him acknowledge that he did wrong in trying to escape God's instruction or in being angry about God's compassion, and he never makes a direct apology to God. Instead, the whole story is a visual representation of sin and repentance, the shape of that spiritual journey: the sin that carries us away from God, the turning point that sends us back and the inevitability of God's mercy when we arrive. And within it, reinforcing those themes, we have the pictures of the repentant Ninevites, the worm destroying the plant and Jonah's annoyance with the character of God being so predictable that even the Ninevites are forgiven. The book of Jonah is about the history of all humanity as much as it is about one person in one time and place.

A question

How concerned are you about the world, in which there are more than 120,000 people who do not know their right hand from their left, and also many animals?

A prayer

Lord, you made me to run on your love. A longing for you is at the root of me. In the ebb and flow of my life, be my homing place, always bringing me back into your compassionate welcome. Amen

The prodigal son: the pigs

> When he had spent everything, a severe famine took place throughout that country, and he began to be in need. So he went and hired himself out to one of the citizens of that country, who sent him to his fields to feed the pigs. He would gladly have filled himself with the pods that the pigs were eating; and no one gave him anything. But when he came to himself he said, 'How many of my father's hired hands have bread enough and to spare, but here I am dying of hunger! I will get up and go to my father, and I will say to him, "Father, I have sinned against heaven and before you; I am no longer worthy to be called your son; treat me like one of your hired hands."'
>
> LUKE 15:14–19

The longest parable told by Jesus is that of the prodigal son, which, like Jonah, is a story that offers a picture of sin, repentance and forgiveness. In it, Jesus uses the visual imagery of a physical distance to represent sin, as well as the idea of a break in a relationship between father and son.

The story begins with the youngest of two sons demanding his share of the inheritance and leaving his father's house to travel to a distant country, where he spends all the money on 'dissolute living' (v. 13), a phrase that reflects what a great and practised storyteller Jesus is. Not saying more about what the son got up to allowed Jesus' audience to supply the details with their own imaginations, which would have keyed straight into both their own prejudices and their own 'dissolute' preferences. A good way to get all his listeners invested in the tale and to make it personal. But – just like the Ninevites in the book of Jonah – the focus is not on the specific sinful actions of the younger son, but on his distance from his father's house. Once again, the simple definition of sin is moving out of relationship with God.

Once the money runs out, the prodigal son finds himself hungry and helpless in a foreign land where the only work he can get is degrading and dirty. The freedom apparently offered by the decision to move away from his father was an illusion. In fact, the son realises, even the servants in his father's house are treated better than he is as a free agent in this distant land. Jesus, still the great storyteller, adds the poignant detail that the son wishes he could eat the pigs' food, but nobody gives him anything for himself: even the animals here have it better than he does.

The turning point for the prodigal is his hunger, rather than his guilt. Instead of remorse for the way he has treated his father or for the waste of his inheritance, his lightbulb moment comes because he is starving and he knows that at home there would be food even for a hired hand. He doesn't expect forgiveness from his father – at least, he doesn't imagine that he will be restored to his previous position by returning – but he does trust his father's grace enough to think that he might have a chance of becoming a servant, so he rehearses a speech in which he confesses that he has sinned and calls himself unworthy. His is not the grateful, trusting path to salvation that we saw in Jonah's prayer; it's a sad, remorseful trudge towards a worse life than he had before – until his father meets him on the road.

When talking about this parable, we tend to look for examples in real life of people who have stories of going to the extremes: people who have turned their backs on family and church in a big way, perhaps gone through the horrors of alcohol or drug dependence, reached rock bottom and cried out to God. But finding a real-life parallel means that we stop applying the story to ourselves. While the parable of the prodigal son can describe a whole life, it equally applies to a journey that happens multiple times a day in the life of any Christian. We make a choice: a half-lie, a task left undone, a click on a tempting advertise-ment that we know will be unhelpful. It's never anything huge, is it?

Avoiding the too-talkative lonely woman after church, grabbing the last seat on the train for ourselves. A tiny act of rebellion. When we go through with it, we find ourselves surrounded by the pigs of guilt, of frustration with ourselves and of hopelessness. Those pigs are greedy and will eat all our joy if they can. They will gobble up the affirmation, the comfort and the self-worth that we were looking for when we did whatever it was that brought us here. We realise, yet again, that those things are found only in God and that we are hungry for the real thing, not the pig-food version. We take a reluctant step back towards doing the hard task, resisting the temptation, correcting the lie. The first few steps often feel as if we're heading back towards servitude; but the more often we take them, the sooner we recognise the father waiting for us on the road.

A question

What are you hungry for?

A prayer

Father, I am sorry for all the times, big and small, that I have headed for the pig pen. I'm sorry for the choices that turn me away from you. I am hungry for things that only you can provide. Please keep bringing me home. Amen

The prodigal son: while we were still far off

But while he was still far off, his father saw him and was filled with compassion; he ran and put his arms around him and kissed him. Then the son said to him, 'Father, I have sinned against heaven and before you; I am no longer worthy to be called your son.' But the father said to his slaves, 'Quickly, bring out a robe – the best one – and put it on him; put a ring on his finger and sandals on his feet. And get the fatted calf and kill it, and let us eat and celebrate; for this son of mine was dead and is alive again; he was lost and is found!'

LUKE 15:20–24

'While he was still far off.' Of all the words and images in the parable of the prodigal son, this phrase has wriggled free from the story and echoed down the centuries with a life of its own. It made its way into the Communion service, and for those like me with liturgy in their blood, this phrase in the story now sparks its interpretation in the post-Communion prayer: 'When we were still far off, you met us in your son and brought us home.'

But what does it mean to be 'far off' from a God who is everywhere? Psalm 139 (which in the NRSV is subtitled 'The Inescapable God') points out that there is nowhere to flee from God's presence: he is in heaven and Sheol and the farthest limits of the sea (vv. 8–9), as Jonah found out in his attempt to escape. The story of the prodigal son provides an essential understanding, both for the beautiful post-Communion prayer and for how God's relationship with human beings has always worked.

My daughter went through a phase of running away from home when she felt things weren't going her way. (So did I. I can still remember the door-slamming rage of it, followed by the sudden realisation that I had nowhere to run to.) I remember her leaving once in high dudgeon, dragging a huge, ripping paper bag full of her favourite soft toys and clutching a banana for the journey. She announced that she was going to find another family to live with, and set off.

We couldn't safely let her wander off into the village unaccompanied, but going with her openly or trying to bring her back only increased her upset. So instead I followed at a distance, ducking behind trees if she looked over her shoulder, like a cartoon spy. She marched off, found a bench, ate her banana and then seemed a little less certain, but she kept going, heading for the playing field – about as far away from our house as she could go without leaving the village. On the field, however, people were walking their dogs. My daughter was terrified of dogs. One look and she swivelled to run back the way she had come, and was relieved to race straight into my arms.

At the phrase 'While he was still far off, his father saw him' (v. 20), we could picture the father sitting at home, gazing longingly out of a high window at the empty road, ready to race off at the first sight of his son returning. But I imagine him following the younger son at a distance, hiding behind trees; and the moment the son makes the decision to set off for home, there is his father, arms open, running towards him.

Both in this story and in the book of Jonah, where journeying away is a metaphor for sin, the moment of meeting with God again does not take place all the way back at the starting point. Instead, it takes place at the moment of turning back. God sends the fish to pick Jonah up from the bottom of the sea; the father comes running to meet his son while he is still far off. From the moment of turning back, there is still a long journey, but God and the one who has rebelled travel back together.

I think that this reflects that wonderful passage in Romans 8:38–39:

> For I am convinced that neither death, nor life, nor angels, nor rulers, nor things present, nor things to come, nor powers, nor height, nor depth, nor anything else in all creation, will be able to separate us from the love of God in Christ Jesus our Lord.

Just as we are reassured in Psalm 139, the love and presence of God are inescapable, no matter where we go or for how long. It is only a human being's own rebellion, a human choosing to turn away, that can create the effect of a distance between them and God. Only sin causes it. The moment we turn back, God is there right behind us, welcoming us. We may be far off; we may have a great distance to go in terms of our choices or our understanding. But whatever the distance, God will travel it with us and bring us home.

A question

Have you ever been far off? Where are you now?

A prayer

Father, sometimes I have spent far too long telling myself that the distance between us is too great, that I will never be able to find my way back to you. In those moments, help me to remember that I don't have to make the long journey home by myself; all I have to do is turn around. Amen

End of section questions

- Which images have you found the most helpful for thinking about sin and repentance?
- How would you define sin?
- In today's world, 'sin' can be seen as a confusing, triggering word or as religious jargon. How might the Bible's images for it help with that?
- The stories of Jonah and the prodigal son both contain a similar shape of a journey away from and towards God. Where have you seen that shape in your own life?
- In Jonah, the worm which made the plant wither could be a metaphor for the Ninevites' lack of knowledge of God which led them to commit atrocities and would have led to their destruction. How can we distinguish between the roots of sin and its consequences? Is it helpful to do so?
- What do the stories tell you about the character of God?

II

Images of forgiveness

In part one, we looked at what sin is, what God thinks of it and how human repentance turns us away from wrongdoing and back to God. What happens next? We have seen from the images in Psalm 51 that sin is not a problem that can be solved by humans. David portrayed it as a stain that needs cleaning, utter brokenness, a damaged heart.

In this section, we will look at some scriptural images of God's forgiveness: pictures of the ways in which God deals with the problem of sin.

When we talk about sin today, we often imagine it as originating in human thought or action. In the following images, however, sin is often imagined as a separate agent, something that comes against humans in some way or something that is in the way and can be removed. Perhaps we are supposed to think of sin not as something intertwined with our human identity, but as a common enemy of God and people.

In most of these pictures, sin is imagined as a concrete noun – in other words, an object, something that can be seen, touched and manipulated. That's the job of a metaphor, to make an abstract into something concrete, helping our imaginations to grasp its meaning. I mention this because it's important to remember that sin is a noun. All too often, we try to describe and define it by making it into an adjective and looking at what is sin*ful*. But that is like trying to define heat by listing things that are hot. If I tried to define heat by describing an oven, a candle flame or the sun, I would be telling you some of the effects of heat, and I might get distracted by questions of which things are more or less hot than others, but I would not have defined heat itself. To do that would probably require a more scientific answer, one which might be harder to understand. In the same way, when we define sin by looking at things which are sinful, we might see some of the effects of sin, but we are also likely to get bogged down in deciding under what circumstances and to what level those things are sinful, and we still won't have explained what sin actually is.

By looking at the images of sin and repentance so far, we have come some way towards working out how to define sin. We have seen that it's a state of being turned away from God, of moving in the opposite direction. Let's see whether imagining sin as a concrete noun, and seeing how God deals with it, helps to shift our thinking and further our understanding.

Sunday

Without leaving a trace

When you stretch out your hands,
    I will hide my eyes from you;
even though you make many prayers,
    I will not listen;
    your hands are full of blood.
Wash yourselves; make yourselves clean;
    remove the evil of your doings
    from before my eyes;
cease to do evil,
    learn to do good;
seek justice,
    rescue the oppressed,
defend the orphan,
    plead for the widow.

Come now, let us argue it out,
    says the Lord:
though your sins are like scarlet,
    they shall be like snow;
though they are red like crimson,
    they shall become like wool.

ISAIAH 1:15–18

One chilly February night, a pair of brothers broke into a property in Bromsgrove, Worcestershire, using a hammer to smash the conservatory windows. They stole some valuable jewellery, a handbag and some money. When it was time to make their exit, one of the brothers took a bottle of cleaning spray and began to cover their traces, erasing fingerprints from anything he thought they had touched. Satisfied that everything was clean, the pair left – leaving behind the spray bottle with a perfect set of prints on it. Of course, the other brother might still have been able to pretend innocence, if it hadn't been for the fact that he had cut himself as he smashed the window, leaving his DNA readily available for the forensic team to find in the resulting bloodstains.

Criminals today must need a degree in forensic science to be able to cover their traces properly. For there to be enough cast-iron evidence against a murderer, they no longer need to be caught red-handed – a phrase which comes, obviously, from finding the perpetrator still stained with the blood of their victim. It's no good protesting your innocence when your hands are covered in blood, and yet that's what the people of Israel are doing in this passage from Isaiah: attempting to engage in prayer and worship as if nothing was wrong, stretching out hands which are 'full of blood'. It's a strikingly visual and visceral image. At the time Isaiah was writing, priests and people had to be ritually clean to engage in worship; here, God is telling them that their clean-up has failed. It is pointless for them to present themselves as clean for worship when they are carrying on with their sin.

These days, bloodstains are important evidence because they contain DNA: both victim and criminal leave a stamp full of details at the scene of a crime. Even before that science was available, the pattern of bloodstains could give lots of information about what had taken place – or at least, that's what detective novels would have me believe. In short, bloodstains are incriminating.

Well before forensic science, though, the evidence given by blood has always been particularly obvious to God. God told Cain that his murdered brother's blood cried out to him from the ground (Genesis 4:10). The voice of Abel's blood in God's ears identified both murderer and victim. Now, in our passage from Isaiah, the stains of violence and evil cover the prayers of God's people so that he cannot listen to them, as if the cries of the blood of their victims drown out the voice of their prayer. Yet it is not just violence which creates this stain, but neglect. God tells them what they should be doing: seeking justice, rescuing the oppressed, defending orphans and pleading for widows. These people who are stretching out their hands to God are also guilty of the blood of those they have not helped. We do not need to have committed violent crimes to share this particular stain.

In verses 15–17 of this passage, God seems to be imploring his people to sort themselves out: 'Wash yourselves; make yourselves clean.' He begs them to stop doing evil and do something good. After all, just as it's no good protesting innocence while still covered in blood, so it's no good saying sorry without also cleaning up your act. These people need a change of heart and a change of direction.

But in verse 18, after the list of things the people should be doing, God takes the responsibility on himself. 'Though your sins are like scarlet,' he promises, 'they shall be like snow.' Just like the image we saw in Psalm 51:7, there is a contrast between the scarlet and crimson of the bloodstains and the whiteness of snow and wool. As in David's psalm, only God can remove those stains without trace; once the people have done their part in repentance, there is still work for God to do before they can finally stretch out clean hands.

And, just as David made reference to the hyssop used to sprinkle sacrificial blood, we know that the scriptural imagery of God cleaning bloodstains tends to involve more blood. In 1 John 1:7, John writes that the blood of Jesus cleanses us from all sin. How does that work? Perhaps the answer lies in the image found in Hebrews 12:24, which describes Jesus as the mediator of a new covenant and says that his blood 'speaks a better word than the blood of Abel'. Blood always gives evidence, but the evidence spoken by the blood of Jesus is different. Instead of crying out to God with accusation, identifying what we have and have not done, the willingly sacrificed blood of Jesus says that we are forgiven and our sins are not held against us. The visual contrast of scarlet and snow is mirrored by an aural metaphor of cries and silence. Through Jesus, we can stretch out clean hands and God will hear our prayer.

A question

When I go to worship, how can I make sure my hands are clean?

A prayer

Lord Jesus, I hold out my hands to you. Please inspect them: show me what I have and have not done. I promise to do my part in changing those things, with your help. Then, Lord, wash away the stains of those things so that I can worship with clean hands and a clean heart. Thank you for your sacrifice for me. Amen

As far as the east is from the west

The Lord is merciful and gracious,
   slow to anger and abounding in steadfast love.
He will not always accuse,
   nor will he keep his anger forever.
He does not deal with us according to our sins,
   nor repay us according to our iniquities.
For as the heavens are high above the earth,
   so great is his steadfast love towards those who fear him;
as far as the east is from the west,
   so far he removes our transgressions from us.
As a father has compassion for his children,
   so the Lord has compassion for those who fear him.

PSALM 103:8–13

We really do have a problem with rubbish on our planet. In 2021, the world contained about 8.3 billion tons of plastic – of which about 6.3 billion tons was rubbish. That number can only increase, as plastic waste doesn't biodegrade and often releases toxic gases as it breaks down into smaller and smaller pieces. A single plastic bottle will take about 450 years to break down completely, but the plastic still doesn't actually go away – it just isn't bottle-shaped any more. It becomes tiny plastic particles in soil, in the ocean, in drinking water. Even when we manage to scoop plastic waste out of the rivers and oceans, we don't have anywhere safe to put it. Wouldn't it be wonderful if somebody could just reach down and take it all far, far away?

What is impossible with plastic is somehow possible with sin – a substance which is just as long-lasting, just as harmful and insidious to the soul as plastic is to the earth. In Psalm 103 – attributed, like Psalm 51, to David – the singer addresses his own soul, telling her to bless the Lord who forgives, heals and redeems her. He paints a picture of God's character as a compassionate father (v. 13) who is slow to anger and full of love.

In verse 10, David writes that God does not repay us according to our iniquities. In a psalm full of assurances of God's steadfast love and forgiveness, our sins and iniquities are still described as something for which we deserve some sort of payment and as something attached or belonging to us: our sins, our iniquities. Earlier in the psalm, David has praised God as one who works justice for the oppressed (v. 6). It is not enough for David to describe God as loving while acknowledging that sin exists; something has to be done about it for us to receive God's love.

In the next two verses, David describes two great distances: that between the heavens and the earth, and the distance between the east and the west. In verse 11, he says that as high as the heavens are above the earth, so great is God's steadfast love towards those who fear him. Beautifully, in describing the enormous distance between earth and heaven, between people and God, David fills that distance with the steadfast love of God, so that we have a picture of God's love bridging the gap between heaven and earth.

Then, in verse 12, David describes the space between the east and the west as the distance that God removes our transgressions from us. As the vertical distance is filled by God's love, the horizontal distance is emptied of human wrongdoing. And these two verses, with their vertical and horizontal planes, form a shape in the imagination. Writing long before Christ, reflecting on God's grace, David describes forgiveness in the shape of a cross: God's love stretching from heaven to earth, sins removed from east to west.

At this point, David is describing not just individual sin, but the sins of a people, and we can read it as describing the sin of all humanity. Through the cross, we look forward to a time when it will all be removed. Not just the ways we have hurt others, but the ways they have hurt us, and the ways in which all people collectively have caused damage, and the reason for it all – all will be lifted away and we will not have to bear any of it any longer.

We really do have a problem with rubbish on this planet, and, sadly, the plastic isn't going to be magically lifted away. The consequences of human sin, in this instance, are plain for all to see in the lasting damage we do to the earth. But what if we thought of sin itself as just as clinging, damaging, toxic and indestructible – just as much of an eyesore, just as filthy as a landfill of plastic waste? Perhaps then we could appreciate the words of this psalm and be filled with gratitude at the prospect that God really does take it all away from us, as far as the east is from the west. We could feel the weight of it lifted off, and know that God sees us and treats us separately from our sin.

A question

If you had to draw 'sin', what would it look like? If you had to draw 'forgiveness', what would you draw?

A prayer

Gracious and compassionate Lord, thank you for your steadfast love. Thank you for taking all this horrible, heavy stuff so far away from me and for seeing me and loving me without it. I know that I can trust you as my compassionate father, who knows me so well that you will always be slow to anger and always full of love. Amen

Tuesday

Underfoot and into the sea

Who is a God like you, pardoning iniquity
    and passing over the transgression
    of the remnant of your possession?
He does not retain his anger forever,
    because he delights in showing clemency.
He will again have compassion upon us;
    he will tread our iniquities underfoot.
You will cast all our sins
    into the depths of the sea.
You will show faithfulness to Jacob
    and unswerving loyalty to Abraham,
as you have sworn to our ancestors
    from the days of old.

MICAH 7:18–20

I once pushed my little sister down the stairs. You might think that's ordinary sibling rivalry, but I wasn't trying to hurt her. I thought that I was saving her life.

We used to spend the summer in a friend's beautiful big house in France. We loved it there, except for the fact that there were several hornets' nests: in the chimney, in the trees outside and in the old stone wall around the garden. As a small girl with an even smaller sister, I got the idea that hornet stings could be fatal to tiny children, so when I saw my sister about to step down on to one of these monsters with her bare feet, I panicked and shoved her from behind. Thankfully, she was more shocked than hurt. I think she forgave me eventually.

There was only one person who could deal with the hornets: my father. He would trap them expertly under a glass with a piece of card, take them to the kitchen table and then dispatch them in a fascinating but somewhat gruesome way which I won't describe here in case anybody is squeamish. Whenever we spotted a hornet indoors, we went running to fetch him.

In these images from Micah, God has dominion over sin in the same way that my father had dominion over the hornets. God is much, much bigger than sin: he is able to tread it underfoot, able to pick it up and throw it. These are images of God stepping in to deal with something we cannot handle by ourselves. The rest of the book of Micah lays out the case against Samaria and Jerusalem in legal language, listing their wrongdoings; but in these final verses, Micah declares that the same God who has been wronged will remove and conquer their sin. The opening of these verses – 'Who is a God like you?' – is a play on Micah's name, which means 'Who is like God?' Micah says that God's uniqueness lies in his ability to pardon iniquity and pass over transgression. He is the only God who can deal with sin without punishing his people.

The image of treading sin underfoot calls to mind the striking picture in Isaiah 63, of a Messiah figure returning from treading a winepress. His clothes are stained with the red juice of the grapes, which becomes a description of blood as it transpires that he has been trampling his enemies – that is, Israel's enemies – in his wrath on a day of vengeance. The passage is a promise and future vision of a day of justice and redemption for Israel.

To tread someone underfoot is to crush and overcome them. In the verses from Micah, however, God treads sin underfoot, rather than the people who have sinned. His vengeance is against sin itself, and so he rescues his people rather than destroying them. Sin is the enemy and not the people he has accused.

In Micah's next image, God casts all our sins into the sea. In biblical imagery, the sea tends to be an image of chaos and forgetting, as well as distance; nobody knows what is in the depths of the sea. We saw this in Jonah's prayer from the fish, when he recalled the bottom of the sea as being like Sheol or the Pit. Jonah was thrown into the sea by the sailors because he was the one who had sinned: sin and sinner alike had to be cast into the sea. But again, when Micah uses the image, only the sin is cast into the sea, leaving the people free of it. God is unique because he is able to separate humanity from sin and destroy the sin alone. Micah's poetry here turns once-violent images of justice and vengeance into symbols of mercy, freedom and hope.

Those words in Micah are written in the future tense. Micah trusts God's compassion and knows his character, but still looks forward to a time when this promise will be fulfilled, when the sins of Israel will be utterly removed and forgotten. He finishes by referring back to the promises given to Abraham and Jacob. Micah is the same prophet who, in chapter 5, foretold the Messiah's birth in Bethlehem. He knew that the one who could crush sin underfoot and cast it into the sea was on his way.

A question

When the day comes, what would you like God to cast into the sea first?

A prayer

Who is a God like you? Thank you, Lord, that you are bigger and stronger than my sin. Amen

Wednesday

Behind God's back

Then the word of the Lord came to Isaiah: 'Go and say to Hezekiah, Thus says the Lord, the God of your ancestor David: I have heard your prayer, I have seen your tears; I will add fifteen years to your life... This is the sign to you from the Lord, that the Lord will do this thing that he has promised: See, I will make the shadow cast by the declining sun on the dial of Ahaz turn back ten steps.' So the sun turned back on the dial the ten steps by which it had declined.

A writing of King Hezekiah of Judah, after he had been sick and had recovered from his sickness...

> Surely it was for my welfare
>   that I had great bitterness;
> but you have held back my life
>   from the pit of destruction,
> for you have cast all my sins
>   behind your back.

ISAIAH 38:4–5, 7–9, 17

Welcome to the wibbly wobbly tale of Hezekiah. What is happening here? Open your Bible to Isaiah 38, step into my time machine and we'll find out.

We are in a royal bedchamber. King Hezekiah, in the middle of a faithfully fought war against the Assyrians, has been laid low by a sudden illness. The prophet Isaiah comes to him with the bad news: God's word is that the king will not recover; he will die. Hezekiah, whose actions and prayers in the last chapter saved the city from the Assyrian onslaught, turns his face to the wall, weeping bitterly, and reminds

God how faithful he has been. Isaiah comes back. He says that God has seen the king's tears and will add 15 years to his life, and as a sign of this, the shadow on the sundial will move backwards, as if time itself is reversing. All eyes look outside to the sundial, and sure enough, the shadow moves by ten steps, as if the setting sun is now rising again.

Has God made the sun rise again? Has time itself shifted? Or has he played with the shadow as a symbol of Hezekiah's extra years, his life's clock turning back from the brink of death? Whichever it is, it is wonderful: a once-in-a-lifetime sight. Hezekiah sits up, feeling better already, and writes a poetic prayer of thanks which is full of the symbols of passing time and the inevitability of death. He plays with images of things happening at the wrong time of day – departing at noontime, wakefulness in the night – to symbolise death as coming at the wrong time. He repeats the line, 'From day to night you bring me to an end' (vv. 12, 13). He pictures a shepherd whose tent is pulled up and packed away while he is still living in it; he writes about a weaver who cuts a cloth down from the loom. All these pictures are of time, of the idea that death has a set time and of things happening outside the right time. And with these images, Hezekiah thanks God for his timely rescue from death and extra 15 years of life.

Then, in verse 17, Hezekiah writes that God has held back his life from the pit of destruction and cast all the king's sins behind his back. My mental image on first reading this phrase was of God hiding sins behind his back the way a naughty child hides a stolen chocolate biscuit. But given all the rest of the time-related imagery, I don't think that this is what Hezekiah meant. Rather, he is saying that God has cast his sins behind him in time; he has left them in the past and looked towards the future, so the sins are behind his back. It's almost as if Hezekiah's sins died when he himself should have died; as if the sins fell into the pit of destruction without him.

Hezekiah finishes his prayer by looking into his new future. 'The living, the living, they thank you,' he writes (v. 19), and he talks about fathers making God's faithfulness known to their children, looking forward with a vision of future generations of living, saved people praising God.

God can manage all of this by being eternal and outside of time as we see it operating. In fact, that's a theme picked up in the next part of Isaiah, when the prophet compares people to grass, but says that 'the word of our God will stand forever' (Isaiah 40:8). Only God can turn back the shadow on a sundial, or the years of a person's life, or the wrongdoings that have already taken place. Little did Hezekiah know it at the time, but only God, in one place and time in history, would cast all the sins of humanity behind his back, turn back the clock on death itself and open the way into a life that lasts forever.

A question

If God could turn back the clock to any time of your life so that you could have another go at it, what time would you choose – or would you rather not?

A prayer

Dear God, thank you that you are so extraordinary, so eternal, that things like time and death and sin are little in your hands. Help me to trust you with them. Amen

Thursday

Sealed up in a bag

O that you would hide me in Sheol,
   that you would conceal me until your wrath is past,
   that you would appoint me a set time, and remember me!
If mortals die, will they live again?
   All the days of my service I would wait
   until my release should come.
You would call, and I would answer you;
   you would long for the work of your hands.
For then you would not number my steps,
   you would not keep watch over my sin;
my transgression would be sealed up in a bag,
   and you would cover over my iniquity.

JOB 14:13–17

This place is not a place of honour. No highly esteemed deed is commemorated here. Nothing valued is here. What is here was dangerous and repulsive to us. This message is a warning about danger. The danger is still present, in your time, as it was in ours. This place is best shunned and left uninhabited.

These words sound almost scriptural, don't they? They certainly sound ancient. An inscription on a Viking place of execution, perhaps, or a curse on an ancient Egyptian temple. In fact, these words were written in 1993 as a proposed message to mark a nuclear waste disposal site. The message, however it was eventually communicated, would have to surpass language and still be visible hundreds of thousands of years in the future – longer than any artefact from any human civilisation has ever survived – because the nuclear waste buried deep underground would still be lethal even then.

It was these words that first sprang to mind when I read Job's wish that his transgressions could be 'sealed up in a bag' and covered over. Like sealed nuclear waste buried deep and covered over by the earth, Job imagines his sin so well hidden that God will no longer keep watch over it.

Job's words come at the end of a passage in which he imagines himself long dead, buried and forgotten. Having lost all his loved ones, he is musing on the finality of human death. 'For there is hope for a tree,' he says dolefully, 'if it is cut down, that it will sprout again... But mortals die, and are laid low' (Job 14:7, 10). I can't help reading it in an Eeyore voice, but after everything that has happened to Job, his depression is certainly understandable.

He then imagines and proposes a solution to this state of affairs which is remarkably close to Christian belief in a bodily resurrection. Hide me in Sheol, he suggests to God, until the unknown reason for all this horror has passed, and then at some preordained time – set your divine alarm clock – remember me, and come and call me back out! Poignantly, he imagines God longing for the work of his hands; a flashback, perhaps, to a time when Job felt loved and valued, safe in the hands of a creator God who now seems distant and cold. I don't mind waiting, Job seems to say, so long as you will miss me eventually.

When I'm at a funeral, I find myself thinking like poor, hopeless, worn-down Job in this passage. Surprisingly – and it does surprise me every time – I find a kernel of faith in myself that is stronger than ever. There is something so horribly final about that coffin being carried out of the church that I can feel the deepest part of my spirit objecting strongly to that finality. It's in those moments that I just *know* the things Jesus said are true, because they are the only answer to the idea that death is the end, and something in me is absolutely convinced that it can't be. Job's reaction to the prospect of his own death is to be able to imagine his resurrection, even though such a thing is not part of his structure of belief. Something in his faithful human spirit just has that hope despite all evidence to the contrary. It's built into us.

But if God called, and Job answered from the grave, then, he reasons, his iniquities would be sealed up in a bag and covered over. Like Hezekiah, Job is aware of the inextricable link between death and sin. Both of them belong to mortality. Everlasting life can't coexist with sin: sin leads directly to death. In Job's imagined resurrection, sin will have to be dealt with, put away, covered over so that it can never be found again, either by God or by Job.

That is why we say that Jesus conquered sin and death. They are so tightly bound up with one another that where one enters, the other floods in. When Jesus returns, we will never go back to them. They will be tightly sealed and covered. Perhaps they will even be marked with a warning?

Nothing valued is here. What is here was dangerous and repulsive to us. This place is best shunned and left uninhabited.

We have been given a far better place to live.

A question

How does your spirit react to death?

A prayer

Lord, sin and death and mortality – it all feels overwhelming, these huge heavy words. We can't focus on them for long without getting bogged down and depressed. Lord, seal it all up. Lock it away. Come back and call us out of it all, and give us the freedom of the day when we won't have to worry about any of it anymore. Amen

Swept away like a cloud

Remember these things, O Jacob,
   and Israel, for you are my servant;
I formed you, you are my servant;
   O Israel, you will not be forgotten by me.
I have swept away your transgressions like a cloud,
   and your sins like mist;
return to me, for I have redeemed you.
ISAIAH 44:21–22

Many holidays spent in the Pyrenees meant plenty of mountain walks together as a family. We had our favourite routes and spots, and every so often we would try something new, maybe a little bit more advanced as my sister and I got older. One holiday, we decided to reach a little peak called the Granquet, which sat majestically above our favourite picnicking spot.

We made several attempts at the Granquet, and in the end our efforts to scale it spanned several holidays. It was always just a little too far for the time we had, or we lost the path and ended up on the wrong side of it, or the weather wasn't right. It became a bit of a joke that the Granquet was determined not to let us climb it. On one occasion, we had the peak in sight when, out of nowhere, a thick mist descended. We decided to keep going – if we followed the path we were on, we would end up in the right place and could wait for the cloud to pass, whereas we could have become hopelessly lost trying to turn back. We reached the place we were sure was the top and were just congratulating ourselves when the mist cleared and we saw the actual Granquet in the near distance, laughing at us.

In our other images so far, sin has been pictured as something so heavy, substantial or immoveable that only God can shift it. Here, the image is of a mist or fog, which at first seems like the opposite: insubstantial and fleeting. But real fog, when you are in the middle of it, can be a serious problem. You can't see anything; you become disoriented, not knowing which is the right way to go. There's a danger of driving off the road or stumbling from the path into a bog. Feeling lost, scared and helpless would seem a good definition of the effects of sin. And, just like the other images, a fog that suddenly appears in the middle of a journey is outside our control. Once again, human beings rely on God as the only one who can deal with sin.

As with the other images of sin, this one points out that sin gets between us and God. Like breath on a window, it obscures our vision, and like mist up a mountain, it can either lead us in entirely the wrong direction or else make us sit down and give up, unable to see a way forward or back.

As well as all that, fog makes it hard for a rescuer to help. It keeps you hidden, even if the search team is quite close. It seems to disperse light and muffle sound, playing tricks on the senses. So it is interesting that in these verses, God promises the people of Israel that he has not forgotten them. The fog of sin may have made them feel unseen, but their rescuer is there. When we lose sight of God through sin or circumstance, it is easy to feel as though God is the one who has lost sight of us. But God has not forgotten us.

God promises to sweep away Israel's sin like a cloud, not just because, being God, he can treat it as if it is as insubstantial as a cloud, but because when it clears, they will be able to see him again. God's promise to sweep sin away is immediately followed by his invitation to return to him. Once the mist has cleared, God's people can return, because now the path is clear and obvious, and the place they ought to have been all along is sitting there in the near distance, inviting them to get up and try again.

A question

What stops you from seeing the way forward clearly?

A prayer

Lord, sometimes I feel obscured by a mist of troubles. I can't see you, and I feel as if you can't see me. Come and sweep away the fog so that I can see my way back to the road home. Amen

Replaced with grace

Then he showed me the high priest Joshua standing before the angel of the Lord, and Satan standing at his right hand to accuse him… Now Joshua was dressed in filthy clothes as he stood before the angel. The angel said to those who were standing before him, 'Take off his filthy clothes.' And to him he said, 'See, I have taken your guilt away from you, and I will clothe you in festal apparel.' And I said, 'Let them put a clean turban on his head.' So they put a clean turban on his head and clothed him in the apparel; and the angel of the Lord was standing by.

ZECHARIAH 3:1, 3–5

My first Girlguiding Brownie meeting, at the age of seven, was a long-awaited event. I dashed excitedly home from school and swapped my school uniform for the brownest pair of trousers I could find, a yellowish T-shirt and a brown knitted cardigan – I wanted to fit in! It had to be gently explained to me that I couldn't wear a Brownie Guide uniform until I had actually become a Brownie. Instead, I had to bear the feeling of sticking out like a sore thumb in my jeans and jumper amid a sea of brown and yellow.

A few weeks later, for my promise ceremony, I proudly donned my smart brown dress (that dates me, for those in the know!), my yellow sash and necker, and the shiny trefoil badge that identified me, at long last, as a real part of this group. More badges, painstakingly sewn on by my mother, revealed to which district, pack and six I now belonged. Although I had been singing the songs, playing the games and sitting in the big circle on the floor of the village hall every week, my clothes had made me stand out as not really a part of it all yet – anybody could have pointed me out as the new girl. But now, making the three-fingered salute and solemnly speaking the memorised words of the Guides' promise and law, I was a Brownie.

Joshua was the high priest in Zechariah's time. In this vision, given by an angel to the prophet, Joshua is standing in the courts of heaven wearing filthy clothes. Satan (which in Hebrew simply means 'the accuser') is pointing him out, presumably accusing him of the sin denoted by what he is wearing. Meanwhile, the angel of the Lord, acting as both defence and judge, rebukes the accuser and replaces the stained garments with new robes.

The role of a high priest was to stand before God on behalf of the people, offering the people's prayers and sacrifices and then pronouncing God's acceptance of them. The filthy robes, therefore, represent the sin of the people, not just of Joshua himself. They combine many of the images for sin that we have already encountered. There's the stain that needs cleaning; the idea of clinging rubbish that needs to be removed and cast away; the picture of something shameful that needs covering.

In this vision, then, we see a process that brings all those images together. Instead of being cleaned or covered up, the filthy robes are removed and taken away altogether. And in their place, Joshua the high priest is given 'festal' robes, ceremonial clothing, which reinstates his position and role.

Joshua's new clothes show that he is accepted, that he is no longer out of place where he stands before the angel of the Lord. They show that he has a role and a purpose there: Zechariah even tells the angels to fetch a priest's turban for Joshua, the one which would have held a gold plate inscribed 'Holy to the Lord' and would have symbolised the people finding favour before the Lord (Exodus 28:36–38).

In this vision, we see that God does not just remove our sin and then leave us, naked and confused, to carry on finding our own way. Instead, he replaces all our sin with his grace, which gives us an identity and a purpose in him and allows us to stand in his court knowing that we are accepted and that we belong there. The badges on our new clothes say things like 'Holy,' 'Righteous' and 'Beloved'. Instead of being ashamed or empty-handed before our accuser, we can point to the robes God has given us as the sign of our belonging. Like a high priest – or a Brownie Guide – we wear our uniform proudly, knowing that every piece of it reminds us that we really are a part of God's kingdom.

A question

What do the badges you wear say about you?

A prayer

Lord, I am standing in your court. I didn't have the right clothes when I came in, but you have robed me in righteousness and clothed me with grace. You have rebuked my accuser and defended me. Thank you, Lord, that I am safe and I belong here with you. Amen

End of section questions

- What difference does it make to think of sin as a noun, rather than a verb that individuals do?
- These images contained a mixture of individual sin and sin that affected a whole community. How does sin affect our communities today?
- In scriptural pictures of God dealing with sin, we have seen sin as being like an object that can be moved, thrown or covered; but it doesn't disappear. Does this tell us something important about sin and forgiveness?
- Do any of these images have echoes in how we talk about what Christ did on the cross?

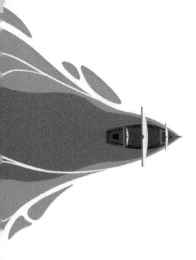

III

Images of atonement

Christians have always believed that the death of Christ on the cross, and his resurrection, solved the problems of sin and death which had been caused by the fall of humanity. Somehow, the death of Jesus has opened the way into everlasting life and achieved atonement – literally, 'at-one-ment', unity and reconciliation – between God and humanity. That much, for most of the church's history, is undisputed.

But there has been plenty of discussion about *how*. From the earliest moments of the church, theologians have been coming up with theories about the mechanism of it all, about what exactly was happening on the grand stage of heaven and earth while Christ was on the cross. These are called atonement theories – and there are many, overlapping and contrasting with one another down the centuries.

This is not a book about atonement theory. However, in one sense, all those theories deal in the same language as this book, in that they almost all begin with an image, a metaphor or a picture found in the

Bible, and develop it into a cosmic theory, a larger picture of how God forgave our sin. In that way, they have the same use that all of the images in this book have: to offer some angles and facets and footholds, some different ways in to thinking about concepts that are too big for humanity to grasp.

In this week of images, we are going to take a look at some pictures and stories that may lie at the root of those atonement theories, so forgive me if I use this introduction for a whistlestop tour of some of them: not because any of the passages we will encounter have an exact parallel with any of the theories, but because they weave in and out of them. A very basic summary of atonement theories might help us to orient ourselves as we look at these central biblical images. And they might help us to find what we are looking for this week, which is to gain some idea of what atonement actually is, what it looks like and what it does.

Possibly the earliest atonement theory was that of *ransom*. The idea was that Adam and Eve sold humanity into slavery, or were captured into it, so that humanity was now owned by the devil. Ransom theory says that with Christ's death as a ransom, God bought us back from the devil.

Following ransom theory came a development of it, *Christus Victor*, in which Christ fought for us and defeated sin and death on humanity's behalf by going through death as both human and God. This was the overriding theory in the medieval church, leading to texts like the 14th-century 'Piers Plowman', in which Jesus fights wearing Piers' armour – in other words, as a human being – to trick the devil into a fight he can't win.

Partly in answer to those theories came the *satisfaction* theory, which argued that God cannot owe anything to the devil – instead, it is sinful humanity that owes a debt to God, which was paid by God himself in Christ's human death.

Penal substitutionary atonement theory introduced the idea of punishment, saying that all sin must be punished and that Jesus took our sin on himself and was punished on the cross instead of us.

No, said the *scapegoat* theory; Christ's death was not punishment, but victimhood: it was God answering human violence by substituting himself for the victims of violence, like the goat that carried away the people's sins into the wilderness.

Meanwhile, in *recapitulation* theory, Jesus is a new Adam, who by leading a perfect life and dying an innocent death, undid the sin and death caused by the first Adam and reset human history.

I haven't listed all of the theories that exist, but you can see how some of the images we've already encountered, and some we are about to look at, flicker around the way that the church has thought and taught about atonement in the past 2,000 years. That's enough of atonement theories. Now let's look at the Bible.

Ransom

If you invoke as Father the one who judges all people impartially according to their deeds, live in reverent fear during the time of your exile. You know that you were ransomed from the futile ways inherited from your ancestors, not with perishable things like silver or gold, but with the precious blood of Christ, like that of a lamb without defect or blemish. He was destined before the foundation of the world, but was revealed at the end of the ages for your sake. Through him you have come to trust in God, who raised him from the dead and gave him glory, so that your faith and hope are set on God.

1 PETER 1:17–21

Even though it wouldn't be my first choice for a cosy evening in front of the television, I'm familiar enough with the following crime drama scenario. A white van drives down a dark street. The person walking on the pavement spots it over his shoulder and breaks into a jog, but he isn't fast enough. The van slows just enough for the doors to open and masked people to jump out: they fall on the hapless pedestrian and, in one smooth movement, put a bag over his head and scoop him into the van. The next day, the letters start arriving, words cut out of magazines and newspapers and stuck on to an old paper bag. They demand a colossal price for the return of the kidnapped person, to be delivered at a neutral spot on a named date, and certain death if any attempt is made at rescue or arrest. When the time comes, a nervous, desperate person climbs shakily out of a car, clutching a suitcase full of cash, and hands it over for the safe release of their loved one.

There are all sorts of reasons for kidnap, and all sorts of demands. We once attended a church where baby Jesus was kidnapped from the crib scene on Christmas Eve. It turned out that the person who had donated the scene many years before was not happy with the church's upkeep of the figures and was refusing to give Jesus back until they had been fully restored.

So what is happening in this image of ransom from the first of Peter's letters? Who is the kidnapper, whom have they captured and what is the ransom demanded for release?

Peter says that the Christians he is writing to were ransomed 'from the futile ways inherited from your ancestors' (v. 18). There, then, is our kidnapper – not the ancestors themselves, but their futile ways, the things they did or believed. It is unclear whether Peter was writing mainly to Jews or to Gentiles: his letter is addressed to scattered, persecuted followers of Christ, and perhaps identifying these ancestors or exactly what they did is not important. Christians reading these words today can all agree that we have been ransomed from the futile ways of our ancestors, from the ways, actions and beliefs of all human ancestry. It is simply another way of saying sin. Sin is the kidnapper.

What is the ransom demanded by sin? As we discovered in the previous chapter, sin leads to death almost seamlessly, so that where one is mentioned the other follows on logically. Sin does not demand a suitcase full of cash; sin wants a body. The ransom paid is not silver and gold, but the blood of Christ.

Peter uses an extra word when he mentions the silver and gold: they are perishable. In those television shows I mentioned earlier, at the point when the suitcase is handed over, there is generally a sudden commotion as special agents who have been disguising themselves as bushes and statues leap out of their hiding places to overcome the kidnapper, while the camera cuts to equally tense scenes in which others are rescuing the victim. Handing over the money is a last resort, because it won't be enough to satisfy the kidnapper. For as long as they are the person with the upper hand, they will be able to keep demanding more and more. Money doesn't last, either as a solution or in the hands of a greedy criminal. In contrast, the ransom that Christ paid for us is imperishable. Sin cannot keep us captive, and it can never demand anything else. Christ's ransom lasts forever.

A question

What would you pay as a ransom for the person you love the most? And how about you – what are you worth?

A prayer

Thank you, Lord, for paying my ransom with your priceless, everlasting blood. Amen

Monday

David and Goliath

When the Philistine drew nearer to meet David, David ran quickly towards the battle line to meet the Philistine. David put his hand in his bag, took out a stone, slung it, and struck the Philistine on his forehead; the stone sank into his forehead, and he fell face down on the ground.

So David prevailed over the Philistine with a sling and a stone, striking down the Philistine and killing him; there was no sword in David's hand. Then David ran and stood over the Philistine; he grasped his sword, drew it out of its sheath, and killed him; then he cut off his head with it.

When the Philistines saw that their champion was dead, they fled.

1 SAMUEL 17:48–51

The story of David and Goliath has made its way into popular language and culture, and no wonder: it really is a great story. Giant, armour-clad, spear-wielding Goliath faced with tiny, youngest-of-eight, five-smooth-stones David is such an evocative image. The story in 1 Samuel is so grippingly told, too, with wonderful details: the boy David being scorned by his brothers when he turns up with their packed lunch; helpless king Saul and the giant with a spear like a weaver's beam; David unable to move under Saul's armour, taking it all off again and heading out with his sling; the insults that Goliath flings at David before David flings a stone at him and topples him in one go. It's another one of those stories that we think we know because we've heard it since we were children. It's always worth going back to the Bible and reading the whole tale from the source again.

Goliath was humiliating Israel. Instead of letting the two armies fight a fair war, Israelites against Philistines, his challenge to one-on-one combat had frozen the battle and kept the Israelite soldiers in their camp. For 40 days, Goliath came out and openly mocked them, confident in the knowledge that they could not provide a man as strong as himself. Every one of his daily appearances brought more shame when a rival representative failed to appear. The Israelites needed a champion.

David may have been comically small next to the giant, but he wasn't weak. He had fought lions and bears while looking after his sheep; he knew that he had strength and technique. What he knew most of all, though, was that this Philistine could not stand against the army of the living God. If the army of the living God was only David, well then, Goliath could not stand against David.

Goliath was disdainfully amused by David's appearance: 'Am I a dog, that you come to me with sticks?' (v. 43). He added mockery, threats and curses. David's calm reply was that he would kill Goliath 'in the name of the Lord of hosts… so that all the earth may know that there is a God in Israel' (vv. 45–46). Goliath was fighting to represent the Philistines; David was representing not just God's people, but God himself.

'When the Philistines saw that their champion was dead, they fled' (v. 51). No further battle was necessary. David had fought successfully on behalf of the whole Israelite army, and won.

In this story, the very beginning of the career of Israel's greatest king, is hidden a picture of that king's greatest descendant. Jesus, like David, appeared against an enemy whose mocking challenge and accusations heap shame on all humanity. Our accuser is powerful, never to be conquered by any mere human; but Jesus, although he was human and appeared weak, possessed unconventional strength which equipped him to fight on our behalf. Neither David nor Jesus had the appearance of a great warrior, but both of them had already been chosen before the time of their battle and anointed: David as the next king; Jesus as the Messiah, the Christ (both of which mean 'anointed'). Just as David represented God as well as Israel, Jesus went to the cross, both human and divine, to represent both God and humanity in his defeat of sin and death.

There's even a little bit of the trickery inherent in *Christus Victor* in the story of David. Fourteenth-century thinkers and poets enjoyed imagining that Jesus' disguised divinity tempted Death into a fight that Death couldn't win, that he somehow took the enemy by surprise by fighting in human armour, and, dying, used Death's own power against him. David, having enticed Goliath out to fight with him thinking that it would be an easy victory, took him by surprise and then cut off Goliath's head with the giant's own sword. It has a flavour of Jesus defeating death by dying: ending all death, forever, with his own death.

Yes, it's no wonder we love the story of David and Goliath. It really is a great story. However, when we tell or hear a great story, we inevitably imagine ourselves as the hero, because that is how stories work. Since childhood, lots of us have been David, bravely whirling a sling against the giants of sin and despair. What if we don't have to fight any more?

A question

What if you don't have to fight any more?

A prayer

Jesus, thank you for standing against the giants of sin and death and defeating them for me. Thank you that their armies fled when they saw that you had killed their champions. Thank you that I can be a part of that triumph without having to fight an impossible battle alone. Amen

Debt

Jesus spoke up and said to him, 'Simon, I have something to say to you.' 'Teacher,' he replied, 'speak.' 'A certain creditor had two debtors; one owed five hundred denarii, and the other fifty. When they could not pay, he cancelled the debts for both of them. Now which of them will love him more?' Simon answered, 'I suppose the one for whom he cancelled the greater debt.' And Jesus said to him, 'You have judged rightly.' Then turning towards the woman, he said to Simon, 'Do you see this woman? I entered your house; you gave me no water for my feet, but she has bathed my feet with her tears and dried them with her hair. You gave me no kiss, but from the time I came in she has not stopped kissing my feet. You did not anoint my head with oil, but she has anointed my feet with ointment. Therefore, I tell you, her sins, which were many, have been forgiven; hence she has shown great love. But the one to whom little is forgiven, loves little.' Then he said to her, 'Your sins are forgiven.'

LUKE 7:40–48

Imagine the scene: you have invited Jesus for dinner at your house. A great deal of time, thought and money has gone into preparing for his visit, and you have been looking forward to finally getting him to yourself and asking all the questions you have stored up. You're not absolutely sure he's going to turn up until you hear the knock at the door, but he comes in as promised and sits down at your table. The dinner is going well, but then you hear somebody else come through the door – Jesus must have left it open behind him – and when this person appears, your heart sinks. You know her. Everybody knows her. She is notorious in your community for her degrading lifestyle, for being disruptive and disreputable. You're a little bit scared of her, to be honest, but it's not you she wants – she goes straight to Jesus and starts making a scene, flinging herself at him, crying all over him. You can't help the expression of disgust on your face as you wonder how you're going to deal with this, and why on earth Jesus is letting this woman carry on like that – where is her dignity? Where is his? Jesus looks up, and instead of addressing the woman, he talks to you. He says he wants to tell you a story.

It's a simple story about two people who owed sums of money – one a large amount, one small. Neither one of them could pay, so both of them were let off their debt. Which one of them is the most grateful?

In this short parable, Jesus draws a direct parallel between debt and sin. In his metaphor, having sinned is like owing a debt to God, with the debts increasing the more the sin is repeated. Receiving God's forgiveness is like being let off the debt, so that the greater the forgiven debt, the more relieved the debtor will be and the more grateful they will be that the debt has been cancelled. Is that all there is to it?

Jesus explains to his host, Simon the Pharisee, that this woman who has come in and poured precious ointment on Jesus's feet has been forgiven many sins; therefore she is showing him much love. In this way, Jesus reframes the woman's sin as an opportunity for great forgiveness and great gratitude. Her sin has been transformed from shame into an opportunity to proclaim God's goodness.

This is not the only time that Jesus uses the same metaphor in a parable. Another example can be found in the parable of the unforgiving servant, in which a servant is forgiven a huge debt by the master, but then insists on the repayment of a tiny debt from a fellow servant, causing the master to throw him into jail and reinstate his debt.

In both parables, there are two debtors. In both, the debts are contrasted as one big and one small. In both parables, neither debtor is able to pay their debt, and so both explore the idea that God's forgiveness is like being let off a debt that cannot be paid. The fact is that, despite the amounts, the two debtors are in exactly the same position as one another.

Perhaps Simon the Pharisee, listening to this parable about the real-life example taking place in his own house, understands Jesus as saying that this woman, whose sins were great, was sure to be hugely grateful when they were forgiven. But he may be missing the fact that, despite their difference in lifestyles, he is just as much in need of forgiveness as the woman at Jesus' feet. He is also a debtor who cannot pay, no matter the amount. Why, then, is he not grateful as well? Jesus' parable points out that the difference between Simon and the woman is not so much the extent of their sin, but their awareness of their need to be forgiven and the gratitude that they show when they learn that it is possible.

You sit at your dinner table. You watch the scene unfold between Jesus and this chaotic woman. You hear him tell her that her sins are forgiven, that her faith has saved her and that she can go in peace. You hear the grumbling of the other important teachers and guests at your table, pointing out that only God can forgive sins: who does this man think he is? You look at Jesus. He looks back at you. It's an invitation, or perhaps, a challenge.

A question

On a scale between Simon and the woman, how grateful are you?

A prayer

Lord, I could never have paid my debt, but you have forgiven it. Thank you – thank you so very much. Amen

Wednesday

The just judge

But now, irrespective of law, the righteousness of God has been disclosed, and is attested by the law and the prophets, the righteousness of God through faith in Jesus Christ for all who believe. For there is no distinction, since all have sinned and fall short of the glory of God; they are now justified by his grace as a gift, through the redemption that is in Christ Jesus, whom God put forward as a sacrifice of atonement by his blood, effective through faith. He did this to show his righteousness, because in his divine forbearance he had passed over the sins previously committed; it was to prove at the present time that he himself is righteous and that he justifies the one who has faith in Jesus.

ROMANS 3:21–26

Frank Caprio, a judge in Providence, Rhode Island, became famous when videos from his courtroom – for a small local TV show filmed by his brother – went viral on the internet. The show, *Caught in Providence*, now has 300 million viewers, all apparently fascinated by real-life footage of parking ticket fines and traffic violation proceedings. Of course, it is not the legal details of the cases that the viewers enjoy, but the character of Caprio himself, because he is a rarity: a merciful judge. Always taking time to listen to the often heart-rending stories behind the repeated parking fines and speeding tickets, he compassionately does whatever he can to help: sometimes giving extra time to pay, sometimes halving or cancelling the fine and sometimes using a court fund, donated to by viewers, to pay the fines on behalf of the defendants.

In this passage from his letter to the Romans, Paul has set up a picture of God as a just judge in a courtroom where every defendant is guilty. In yesterday's picture of debt, no matter how much money was owed, the debtors were all unable to pay. In the same way, Paul points out here that there is 'no distinction, since all have sinned and fall short' (vv. 22–23). The only way for any human to plead is guilty.

But, Paul says, we are now justified by God's grace 'as a gift'. Like the people who come to Frank Caprio's court, we will find ourselves unpunished and walking free, even though we owed the fine by law; somebody else has freely given their own money and paid the ticket for us.

Imagine, though, that rather than having a fund of viewers' donations, Frank Caprio paid all the fines himself in full. Imagine that, as well as the fines, he took on any other punishment required by law for anybody that came through his court: community service, prison sentences, even the death sentence, in the place of all those strangers. And imagine that, rather than a string of single mothers and hard-working carers with heart-breaking excuses, the defendants included depraved criminals who had done terrible deeds with malice aforethought.

I wonder whether that show would get so many viewers? Possibly not, but it does give us a better idea of what Paul is describing to the Romans. The gift of grace that justifies us is Christ's sacrifice of atonement. The just judge takes on the punishment of all humanity – even the sin, says Paul, that had been passed over before due to God's forbearance. There is a new plea in the courtroom: those who have faith in Jesus are justified.

Three hundred million viewers tune in to *Caught in Providence* for entertainment. I wonder how many of them have ever stood in a courtroom themselves? When I watch a show like that, I often find myself judging alongside the judge, thinking, *This one seems guilty*, or, *That's a reasonable excuse*, and deciding that he should let that person off but not this one. I suspect, if we are honest with ourselves, that's how we first imagine God's courtroom as well: as if we are seeing it as a spectator. We sit in the gallery, thinking that some of our fellow humans are less deserving than others, that some sins are bigger or smaller than others, that we wouldn't have done that or made that mistake. How often do we picture ourselves standing in the dock and realise that there is no distinction, that we are guilty too?

A question

How do you react to the judge's verdict? Will your reaction be the same for others as it is for yourself?

A prayer

Lord, you are the only just judge. Thank you for letting me walk free from your courtroom, for taking my punishment for me. Help me to leave the judgement of others to you. Amen

The high priest

Furthermore, the former priests were many in number, because they were prevented by death from continuing in office; but he holds his priesthood permanently, because he continues forever. Consequently he is able for all time to save those who approach God through him, since he always lives to make intercession for them.

For it was fitting that we should have such a high priest, holy, blameless, undefiled, separated from sinners, and exalted above the heavens. Unlike the other high priests, he has no need to offer sacrifices day after day, first for his own sins, and then for those of the people; this he did once for all when he offered himself. For the law appoints as high priests those who are subject to weakness, but the word of the oath, which came later than the law, appoints a Son who has been made perfect forever.

HEBREWS 7:23–28

Several times during the Covid-19 pandemic, we had the misfortune of having to do home tests for coronavirus for the whole family. We found we had to put aside about half a day if we wanted to follow the instructions to the letter, especially the parts regarding cleanliness. First, you wash your hands. Then you clean a surface. Then you wash your hands again, because you've touched the sponge that wiped the surface. You get out all the fiddly little bits of kit, lay them out on your clean surface and blow your nose. Then you wash your hands again, because you've blown your nose. At last, you actually do the test, and then you wash your hands again. Repeat the entire process for two children. Then, if it's the type of test that gets sent off to a lab, you pack each one into its individual postage box, then wash your hands, sanitise the box, wash your hands again, and go to post it. And when you get home, make sure you wash your hands…

Pandemic levels of cleanliness are rivalled only by the instructions given in Leviticus 16 for the high priest to make atonement. Aaron had to wash before he put on the holy vestments. Before he could make atonement for the people, he first had to do so for himself and his house, offering a bull as a sin offering. He then had to make atonement for the sanctuary, the tent of meeting and the altar itself, so that all these were purified enough to receive the sin offering for the people. Only then could he make atonement for the people with the scape-goat (which we'll find out more about tomorrow). After that ceremony, Aaron had to take off his vestments and wash, then put the vestments back on before presenting the burnt offerings. And the people who had helped with the animals also had ritual washing to do before they could come back into the camp.

The consequence of not doing all this properly, in the correct order, was death. The presence of God in the holiest place, inside the curtain, was too overwhelmingly powerful, and the introduction of any trace of sin into that presence was cataclysmic. Aaron knew about that: he had lost two sons when they got it wrong.

All these precise instructions are a picture for us of our need for a perfect high priest. How could any human being ever make a full atonement for all people in the presence of God? The best and most practised of them could barely stay alive; the window of sinlessness could not stay open for any longer than the ceremonies. That's what the writer of Hebrews explains so clearly, pointing to Jesus as our perfect and permanent high priest. Because he has everlasting life, he holds his position everlastingly. Because he is sinless, he does not need to make sure that he has atoned for his own sins before he can start doing so for others. Most of all, because he himself is the sacrifice, he does not need to offer them over and over again, with each one losing its effect; his own presence in the holiest place in heaven is enough, once and for all.

The worst thing about housework is the way you have to keep on doing it. I can never be satisfied with a shiny kitchen for long: by the time I've finished cleaning it, it's time to make the next meal, and then the surfaces are covered and the pans and plates are dirty and it all needs cleaning again.

That is just what life is like, isn't it? Next time you are picking things up off the floor that you only tidied an hour ago, or washing the car that went through a muddy puddle six feet outside the carwash, think about Aaron peeling off all of his vestments to wash and then putting them all back on again and getting back to the sacrifices. Imagine what he might have said when he finally met Jesus; and say your own prayer of thanks for the once-for-all that put an end to the constant, repetitive weariness of it all and allowed us to come into the presence of God without fear, through our perfect, everlasting great high priest.

A question

How can we keep our awareness of everything that Jesus has spared us from? What will be the things that remind you today?

A prayer

Lord Jesus, you are our great high priest, who once and for all did the work required to stand before your Father in heaven. Thank you for being in that place for me. Thank you that I can come to you without preparation and without fear. Help me to keep remembering why that is. Amen

Friday

The goat for the wilderness

Since, then, we have a great high priest who has passed through the heavens, Jesus, the Son of God, let us hold fast to our confession. For we do not have a high priest who is unable to sympathise with our weaknesses, but we have one who in every respect has been tested as we are, yet without sin. Let us therefore approach the throne of grace with boldness, so that we may receive mercy and find grace to help in time of need.

HEBREWS 4:14–16

As part of the atonement ceremonies in Leviticus 16, Aaron the high priest was told to take two goats and draw lots between them. One goat would be selected 'for the Lord' and the other for the scapegoat. The first goat would be sacrificed as a sin offering, but the second goat remained alive. After doing the first round of cleansing and atonement, Aaron would lay his hands on the head of the scapegoat and confess the sins of all the people, transferring them to the goat: then the goat would be led out into the wilderness. Leviticus 16:22 explains: 'The goat shall bear on itself all their iniquities to a barren region; and the goat shall be set free in the wilderness.'

We have seen, again and again in all the metaphors so far, that the consequences of sin are death and distance, and we see that again in the symbolism of the two goats: one killed, the other exiled. There is a little echo, perhaps, of the story of Cain and Abel, the two sons of Adam and Eve: Abel was dedicated to the Lord and was killed; Cain was guilty of his murder and exiled. It's a pattern that repeats in other tales of biblical brothers, in particular Abraham's two sons Ishmael and Isaac: Isaac was for the Lord and Ishmael for the wilderness. The two goats of the atonement take the place of Israel and suffer death and distance in their place, one for the Lord, one for the wilderness.

The writer of Hebrews, exploring the picture of Jesus as our one great high priest, points out that he is able to sympathise with our weaknesses, because he was tempted, just like us, but without sin. This is true of Jesus' whole life, but it also happened in a specific time and place: in the wilderness. Straight after he had been baptised – a symbolic cleansing and purifying – Jesus, like the scapegoat, went into the wilderness. Like the scapegoat, which was supposed to starve to death eventually, he fasted from food and drink. There, in the wilderness, he was tempted with three very human sins. First, he was tempted to turn stones into bread to eat, using his power to help himself. Next, he was told to jump from the temple so that angels would rescue him, using his power to prove himself above human frailty and to glorify himself. Finally, he was shown the whole world and tempted to hand over his power to Satan in order to possess the world. All three temptations are the basis of human sin: to help ourselves first, to glorify ourselves above others and to gain the world by turning from God. In the wilderness, Jesus resisted them all.

Legend has it that a scapegoat once returned, after many months, from the wilderness, which was seen as such a bad omen that the tradition changed from letting the goat wander freely away to starve, to pushing it over a cliff. After all, nobody wants all their sins returning between the horns of a ravenous, angry goat. But Jesus did walk back out of the wilderness, and he did so without any sin at all. Having taken the role of the goat chosen for the wilderness, he came back to face the role of the goat chosen for the Lord – to complete the work of atonement.

The scapegoat was exiled so that the people of Israel could safely draw close to God. The writer of Hebrews tells us that, since Jesus was tested but without sin, we can approach the throne of grace boldly and receive God's mercy there. Neither death nor distance can come between us and God, because we have Jesus as our high priest.

A question

Can you imagine Jesus sympathising with your weaknesses?

A prayer

Jesus, when I think about my weaknesses, I am so glad that you sympathise with them. Thank you for understanding. Thank you for resisting so much, for not giving in to any of those temptations that would have made things easier for you. Give me the strength to follow you as best I can, and thank you for loving me even when I fail. Amen

Saturday

Passover

This is how you shall eat it: your loins girded, your sandals on your feet, and your staff in your hand; and you shall eat it hurriedly. It is the passover of the Lord. For I will pass through the land of Egypt that night, and I will strike down every firstborn in the land of Egypt, both human beings and animals; on all the gods of Egypt I will execute judgements: I am the Lord. The blood shall be a sign for you on the houses where you live: when I see the blood, I will pass over you, and no plague shall destroy you when I strike the land of Egypt.

EXODUS 12:11–13

My friends and I sat on the edges of the bag racks outside the school library: favourite sixth formers' haunt of the breaktime before lunch, close enough to the dining room for us to leap into the queue as it started to move. Today we looked different. Some of us had our school ties around our heads, and all of us had colourful writing all over our white school shirts: signatures and doodles from both friends and teachers. Over in the boarding house, my trunk was packed and the walls of my room, usually colourful with posters, fabric hangings and revision notes, were bare. The wide world of adulthood beckoned us into different universities, gap years and apprenticeships. The familiar school grounds already felt smaller. We were exhilarated and terrified in equal measure. There had been leavers' pranks, and a wonderful list of lasts – the last lesson, the last exam, the last ever hockey game in the rain! – but there had been tears too. A bell rang, the last one that would ever make us leap to attention. The queue started to move, and we crowded in to eat our last meal all together.

The people of Israel ate their Passover meal ready to go: sandals on their feet, coats on, bags packed. They ate in anticipation of release. Imagine the adrenaline that must have accompanied that meal, given the knowledge they had of what was about to happen. It was the event that changed the calendar forever: the instructions for it begin with the words, 'This month shall mark for you the beginning of months; it shall be the first month of the year for you' (Exodus 12:2). This was the start of a new life. The meal immediately became a festival to remember God's rescue, observed from the year that followed it, up until this year and beyond: 'throughout your generations you shall observe it as a perpetual ordinance' (v. 14). In saving the Israelites' firstborn children from death, God was saving future generations, a future people set aside and marked out as belonging to God.

The passover lambs signified a rescue from death, but the Passover itself was part of a bigger rescue, the release of the people from slavery. That night, death swept across Egypt, killing all the firstborn, whether human or animal. Only the houses marked with the blood of the passover lambs were spared: death passed over them. In the middle of the night, as everyone from Pharaoh to the slaves discovered their dead, the Israelites were released from Egypt and left immediately, with only the things they had ready.

That night would open a new chapter in the history of God's people, one that led to the promised land. They were about to embark on a long journey of learning God's faithfulness for 40 years in the wilderness. They did not know that yet, of course. They only knew that the doors were about to open on the prison they had been in, and they would be free.

Christians remember that Jesus' death rescued us, not just from everlasting death, but also from slavery to sin. Jesus even gave us our own last meal to remember our rescue. But do we eat it with our bags packed, our belts tied and our shoes fastened? Are we ready to go? The blood of the lamb does not intend to leave us where we are, or as we are. Its purpose is to move us onwards and outwards, away from our captors, escaping the place where we were enslaved and into a journey where we will learn the faithfulness of God. Are you ready?

A question

What are you leaving behind?

A prayer

Jesus, you rescued us for a new and different life, for a journey, for times in the wilderness as we move closer to the place you promised to us. Don't let me sit still. My bag is packed and my shoes are fastened. It's scary, but I want to follow you out of here, wherever you are going. I'm ready, Lord. Let's go!

End of section questions

- What do you think of the theories of atonement? Are they useful? Are they necessary? Do any of them resonate more than others?
- This week's metaphors have included several images of Jesus: as a judge, a master owed a debt, a soldier, a sacrificial animal, a great high priest. Do any of them stand out to you? Which is the most unexpected? Which is the easiest to imagine? Is it helpful to have so many different metaphors?
- How would you answer the question, 'Why did Jesus have to die?'

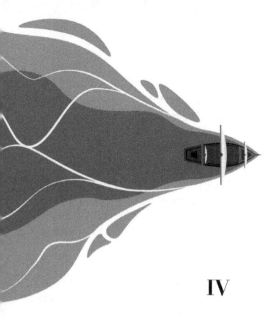

IV

Images of restoration

Forgiveness is not the end of the story. In the past few chapters, we have seen some images of the effects of sin, what God thinks of it and how God deals with it. In this next section, we look ahead to the next step. Forgiveness of sin is a means to an end: just as Job imagined, once sin has been removed from the picture, it opens the way for us to be restored, brought back into God's plan for a perfect world and for peace between God and his people.

This week, we will explore images of what that restoration could look like. How can God take damaged people, in a world splintered by the effects of sin and death, and restore them? What would be the steps towards doing that, and what part does forgiveness have to play in it?

The pictures in this section are all of God renewing and restoring individuals, communities and landscapes. They range from exploring God's creativity as a potter to depicting the painful, even terrifying prospects of a refiner's fire or a heart surgeon. But in all the pictures, it is God doing the work; even once we have been forgiven, we are not expected to carry on in our own strength, to remake or reinvent ourselves. Instead, God is the restorer of his people and his creation.

Unlike forgiveness, however, where dealing with sin is in God's power alone, these pictures have some hints that we are invited to join God in his work of restoration. From Ezekiel being asked to prophesy life to dry bones to Paul's description of Christians as heaven's ambassadors and people with a ministry of reconciliation, those who have made peace with God begin to work together with him and with each other to bring about peace on earth.

Just as, at the end of last week, we walked forward into the wilderness after being rescued from slavery, so this week we discover that being forgiven gives us a new role in God's kingdom. Let's work it out together.

The potter's wheel

The word that came to Jeremiah from the Lord: 'Come, go down to the potter's house, and there I will let you hear my words.' So I went down to the potter's house, and there he was working at his wheel. The vessel he was making of clay was spoiled in the potter's hand, and he reworked it into another vessel, as seemed good to him.

Then the word of the Lord came to me: Can I not do with you, O house of Israel, just as this potter has done? says the Lord. Just like the clay in the potter's hand, so are you in my hand, O house of Israel. At one moment I may declare concerning a nation or a kingdom, that I will pluck up and break down and destroy it, but if that nation, concerning which I have spoken, turns from its evil, I will change my mind about the disaster that I intended to bring on it.

JEREMIAH 18:1–8

It is mesmerising to watch a potter working at the wheel. They make it look so easy that the tall vase between their hands seems to grow up of its own accord and take on a beautiful shape. Of course, anybody who has ever tried to throw a pot on a wheel will tell you that it is not easy at all. The clay seems to have a mind of its own, the slightest weight in one place causing it to wobble out of control, the walls of the pot collapsing in on themselves. A beginner might stop the wheel and poke at the mess in dismay, wondering whether any of it can be patched up, but a professional potter just returns the whole thing to blob form and begins again.

God took Jeremiah to the potter's house to show him a metaphor. Whatever the potter was trying to make at his wheel wasn't working, and rather than trying the same thing again, the potter shaped the clay into something different. In the same way, God told Jeremiah, if a nation is heading for disaster, but then repents, God can reform it into something good.

This may not be the comforting message that it seems at first, because God goes on to say that the same applies to a nation that doesn't repent: God, as the potter, is 'shaping evil' against unrepentant, wayward Israel. The picture is a warning: whatever shape the pot may be inclined to take on, the potter is the one in charge.

The striking thing about this picture, though, is that the potter makes a different vessel after the first one is spoiled. Why change from the shape of his first attempt? It's as if the potter's creative decision about the shape of the pot is influenced by the clay in his hands. Instinctively, he guides it into a shape that is best suited to the amount, the texture and the malleability of the clay. If one shape doesn't work, the potter tries another.

The other day, my daughter tried to draw her favourite cartoon character, copying it from the paused screen of her video. When it didn't look right, she became frustrated, pushed the picture aside and started a new one. I had a look at what she had done and, with her permission, I altered the jawline of her character so that suddenly it looked a lot more like the one on the screen. When she saw that my alteration had done the trick, she took the paper back and began working on it again.

God threatens that he is 'shaping disaster' for Israel, but it's interesting that in the picture he shows Jeremiah, the potter does not discard the clay. In fact, he shapes it 'as seems good to him' to make a different pot. It's as if, in a moment of creative frustration, God says that he is ready to destroy his work, but in fact he waits for Israel to repent so that he can carry on shaping the nation.

The pot being 'spoiled' has become a part of its history: it has, in some way, affected the shape it ends up being. Different vessels have different purposes, so the pot's use may also have been affected. But nothing has been discarded. The pot has ended up in a shape that seemed good to the potter. When the wheel stops, it is because the potter is pleased with his work.

Our choices shape our lives: we have free will. We may resist the shaping hands of God the potter, who had an idea and a purpose for us. Outside influences might affect us, too. But at any point, we can give ourselves back to God's creative vision, and God the potter will rescue and restore us, including the disasters that have shaped us, into a new design and a fresh purpose that he considers good. If we trust ourselves to the divine creativity of our maker, he will not stop the wheel until he is happy with the work of his hands.

A question

What has shaped your life?

A prayer

Creative God, you imagine good futures for me, and you shape me for the purposes you have in mind. I am always being designed by you. Let me bend to the guiding of your hands, as seems good to you. Amen

Monday

Heart transplant

The sin of Judah is written with an iron pen; with a diamond point it is engraved on the tablet of their hearts, and on the horns of their altars, while their children remember their altars and their sacred poles, beside every green tree, and on the high hills, on the mountains in the open country.

JEREMIAH 17:1–3

But this is the covenant that I will make with the house of Israel after those days, says the Lord: I will put my law within them, and I will write it on their hearts; and I will be their God, and they shall be my people. No longer shall they teach one another, or say to each other, 'Know the Lord', for they shall all know me, from the least of them to the greatest, says the Lord; for I will forgive their iniquity, and remember their sin no more.

JEREMIAH 31:33–34

I will sprinkle clean water upon you, and you shall be clean from all your uncleannesses, and from all your idols I will cleanse you. A new heart I will give you, and a new spirit I will put within you; and I will remove from your body the heart of stone and give you a heart of flesh. I will put my spirit within you, and make you follow my statutes and be careful to observe my ordinances.

EZEKIEL 36:25–27

These three passages are unconnected, other than in theme; one of them is not even from the same book as the other two. However, putting all three side by side gives us a wide-angle view of the image of a sinful heart, and some of the things they have in common apart from that central image are truly fascinating.

In Jeremiah 17, the prophet, speaking God's words, is describing the depth of the people's sin in God's eyes. He uses the image of an engraving, gouged into the heart of Judah with a diamond-tipped pen made of iron. The image of hardness is there, not in the description of the heart itself, but of the pen needed to write on it: diamond and iron are required to make a mark on the toughest of surfaces. Once something has been engraved so deeply on such a hard surface, it cannot be erased. The image shows how the very action of sin affects the heart: scratching over the same path again and again makes a deeper and deeper impression. The engraving of sin on the hearts of the people matches one on the horns of their altars. They have dedicated themselves to a different god, both in their hearts and with their sacrifices and worship. The sin goes so deep that it has been passed on to their children, who now remember the trappings of idol worship – their altars and sacred poles – instead of the word of God.

Jeremiah 31 is about remembrance too. God offers a new way for his people to remember him, and in return he promises to remember them, renewing their exclusive relationship: he is their God, they are his people. In the first passage, the people of Judah had engraved their own hearts with sin because of their idolatrous actions; here, God promises to be the engraver instead, writing his word on the hearts of his people so that they lean naturally towards God and away from sin. Just as the sin engraved on the heart of Judah led to idolatry, so God's law written on the heart of Israel will lead them back into worshipping God. With Israel remembering God, God promises to forget their sin.

In Ezekiel 36 we find similar images, with one big difference. Once again, the heart connected with sin is led into idolatry: God promises to cleanse the people from all their idols. Once again, the treatment of the heart is a means, not only of forgiveness, but also of a new life which naturally remembers to follow God's statutes instead of leaning towards sin. But this time, instead of writing, the image is of two different hearts: one of stone and the other of flesh.

God offers a complete heart transplant: a heart of flesh given for a hardened heart of stone. This image contains a vulnerability missing from the others. To follow God, our hearts must be softer: more easily wounded, or perhaps more easily moulded, changed, warmed, concerned. In other words, they must be more sensitive to God's call on us. Not only that, but we must be prepared to give up the hearts we had before and all the things they loved and followed. Heart surgery is scary. It is not a quick dose of medicine, but a risky operation for which we will have to trust the hands of the surgeon.

The linking of idols to hearts tells us something else about this image as well. Hearts made of stone lean towards idols made of stone. Remember how the engraving on the heart of Judah matched the engraving on the horns of the altar? Hearts of flesh, on the other hand, seek a person to love and to worship. We follow Jesus, who is God's word made flesh. A heart can know, and love, another heart. Jesus connects our hearts of flesh directly to the heart of God.

A question

What is written on your heart?

A prayer

Father, some of the things my heart loves are very dear to me, but I want you to be the one my heart follows. I trust you to restore or replace my heart so that it inclines towards you and your way. I place my heart in your hands. Amen

Tuesday

The refiner

But who can endure the day of his coming, and who can stand when he appears? For he is like a refiner's fire and like fullers' soap; he will sit as a refiner and purifier of silver, and he will purify the descendants of Levi and refine them like gold and silver, until they present offerings to the Lord in righteousness. Then the offering of Judah and Jerusalem will be pleasing to the Lord as in the days of old and as in former years.

MALACHI 3:2–4

Have you ever seen silver being extracted and refined using ancient methods? I have, just now, and I can't imagine what people writing books like this one used to do before the internet. Anyway, to my completely uninitiated eye, this is what happened in the video I have just watched. A man took a bucket of rubble. He smashed it to make smaller rubble, mixed it with some stuff that would reduce the melting point of metals and placed it in a crucible inside a furnace which he heated to over 1,000 degrees Celsius. Later, he removed the now white-hot crucible with an enormous pair of tongs and poured what looked like lava into a container shaped like an inverted pyramid. Hours later, when it had completely cooled, he removed a black pyramid-shaped rock from the container and used a hammer to smash off the pointy bit, which looked just as black as all the rest to me, but which he said contained the silver that would have sunk to the bottom of the container. He then repeated this process – I lost count of how many times – each time adding a different metal, or scooping oxidised metals off the top of the crucible. And every time he poured the molten metal into the cooler, it looked a little smoother. Eventually, he had a cone of shiny silver, easily discernible from the blacker stuff underneath.

I still have no understanding of the chemistry of it, but from the visuals of this technique, I can grasp the main points of the image that Malachi uses for the coming Messiah, who is both refiner and refiner's fire. The things that stand out to me are the incredibly hot fire, the patience of the refiner, the many stages of the process and, perhaps most importantly of all, the fact that the refiner knew there was silver in his bucket of rubble in the first place.

It's no wonder that Malachi asks who will be able to stand the day of the Messiah's coming. Nothing can withstand fire so hot that looking into the furnace is like peering down into the mouth of a volcano. This process leaves no room for imperfections; every little bit of anything that is not silver will be found and melted away.

It's not just a single process, either. The refiner and purifier of silver in Malachi's image is sitting over a lengthy and complicated business. He knows when to add a metal and when to skim one off; when to heat the mixture and when to cool it. He works patiently, and with every step of the process, the silver becomes a little more recognisable, a little closer to pure.

At the end of the purification process, the offerings of Judah and Jerusalem will be as pleasing to the Lord as they were long ago. They have become contaminated, unrecognisable from the way they were supposed to be, but the Messiah, the refiner, knows that there is silver in there somewhere, hiding in what looks like a bucket of rubble, and he is prepared to put the work in to get it out.

The image of the unrefined silver, mixed in and bonded with other metals in bits of rock, is very like the ones in Jesus' parables about the kingdom of heaven. Weeds grow alongside the wheat; fish are all caught together in a net. Only after the harvest can everything be sorted out, the good saved and the waste burned or thrown away. In the image of purified silver, it is only the skill of the refiner that can separate the silver from the dross, or even know that it's in there to be separated. These are pictures of judgement, of God being the only one who can ultimately judge between good and evil. They also offer a useful way of looking at the problem of pain in our world and answering the question of why God doesn't step in and sort it all out now. Before Jesus comes again, there is no way to pull apart the good from the bad without damaging what is good. Only the refiner's fire can do it.

These pictures tell us that our own judgement may be wrong. We will not always be able to tell good and evil apart as easily as we think we can. We cannot see the silver in the rubble. Even within our deepest selves, we may find that things we thought were shiny were merely fool's gold and the metal of real value is hidden elsewhere. We may find that things we are deeply attached to have no value in the kingdom of God, while things we think of as worthless are prized like fine silver. Can we trust the judgement of the refiner? Can we bear his painful process, which over and over again burns away things we thought would always be a part of us? If we can, we will gradually be restored to a long-forgotten existence, and the refiner will look at us and be pleased.

A question

Looking back, can you see the stages of your restoration? What has already been burnt away?

A prayer

Lord, when I look at the world and other people, help me to remember that I cannot always tell the silver apart from the dross. Show me how tightly intertwined they sometimes are, and give me the wisdom and patience to let you be the one to separate them. Thank you that, one day, your fire will have burned all the dross away. Amen

Like Eden

Thus says the Lord God: On the day that I cleanse you from all your iniquities, I will cause the towns to be inhabited, and the waste places shall be rebuilt. The land that was desolate shall be tilled, instead of being the desolation that it was in the sight of all who passed by. And they will say, 'This land that was desolate has become like the garden of Eden; and the waste and desolate and ruined towns are now inhabited and fortified.' Then the nations that are left all around you shall know that I, the Lord, have rebuilt the ruined places, and replanted that which was desolate; I, the Lord, have spoken, and I will do it.

EZEKIEL 36:33–36

On a bright winter morning, driving back from dropping off my daughter at her new school, I saw an unexpected shape in the sky. I pulled over, stopped the car and gazed up at the huge bird performing aerobatics above my head. The deep forked shape of the tail and the slender cut of its wings told me that this was not one of the buzzards we see frequently over Suffolk fields; this was unmistakably a red kite, and it was majestic.

For most of my early childhood, I would not have been able to see a red kite in England; there were only a handful of breeding pairs in Wales. I learned their distinctive shape on our trips to France, when it was exciting to spot one swooping above a field. Red kites were reintroduced in the Chilterns in the early 1990s, with huge success. There are plenty of parts of England, now, where it is not at all unusual to see flocks of them every day. A friend of mine lives in an area where they are regarded as more of a loud nuisance than anything else. Here in

Suffolk, however, I've only ever seen one a couple of times, and I was thrilled to spot one so close to home. They will always be one of my favourite birds, wherever they appear, but knowing that they came back from the brink of disappearance within my lifetime makes them even more special.

Nature is very good at coming back from the brink. Rewilding projects over the past few years have shown the difference it can make to let over-farmed areas return to their natural state and to reintroduce long-lost species. It turns out that beavers can prevent flooding and that bison naturally coppice woods and provide habitats for smaller creatures to reappear. New growth rebalances the carbon-heavy atmosphere, and the soil becomes richer. Ecosystems run wonderfully well without human interference – almost as if they were designed that way. None of this should be surprising, of course.

In this passage from Ezekiel, God's words spoken through the prophet promise that forgiveness will lead on to the restoration of the land. It's all there in the verbs: inhabited, rebuilt, tilled, fortified, replanted. All this, says God, happens on the same day that the people are cleansed from their iniquities. The forgiveness and the restoration are directly linked. Life flourishes again in places that were desolate, and passers-by say that it looks like Eden.

Eden is not mentioned here just because it's an image of a beautiful garden. God's mention of Eden indicates a restoration, not just of the cities that were built by people, but of the whole world the way it was before the fall: a place of perfect peace, a place where God and humans walked side by side because there was no sin to come between them. This is a picture of humanity restored to relationship with God in a world from which sin has been removed.

Like most prophecy in the Bible, this passage looks forward to more than one place at once, and it speaks to the nation as well as the individual. For every sin repented and forgiven, for every turning of a nation, for every restoration of God's people, there is a little picture of an ultimate future in which every sin will be removed and the whole world restored. For any individual who reaches out to God through Jesus and receives forgiveness, there is a little moment of peaceful Eden to mirror the promised restoration to come – and not just to mirror it, but to bring it closer. Forgiveness leads to Eden, step by tiny step.

Next time you see a red kite, or a plant growing through a crack in the concrete, or a corner of the park turned over to wildflowers, think to yourself, *There's a little bit of Eden*. One day, when God's work of grace is complete, the whole world will be restored.

A question

Where have you seen restoration recently?

A prayer

Heavenly father, show me glimpses of Eden.

Thursday

Dry bones

The hand of the Lord came upon me, and he brought me out by the spirit of the Lord and set me down in the middle of a valley; it was full of bones. He led me all round them; there were very many lying in the valley, and they were very dry. He said to me, 'Mortal, can these bones live?' I answered, 'O Lord God, you know.' Then he said to me, 'Prophesy to these bones, and say to them: O dry bones, hear the word of the Lord. Thus says the Lord God to these bones: I will cause breath to enter you, and you shall live. I will lay sinews on you, and will cause flesh to come upon you, and cover you with skin, and put breath in you, and you shall live; and you shall know that I am the Lord.'

EZEKIEL 37:1–6

God showed Ezekiel a valley full of dry, disconnected, unsorted bones. Imagining the sight makes me think of archaeologists uncovering ancient mass graves in the desert; or the catacombs under Paris, which hold the disconnected skeletons of over six million people; or the charnel houses in cemeteries into which old bones were tossed when they had been exhumed to make space for new graves. Visiting these places, it would not be unusual to have to remind oneself that the bones are human remains: that these bones once belonged to real people who walked and talked, who had names and families. The sheer quantity of them, their age and the way they are arranged in bits and pieces makes looking at them feel more like viewing an artwork or some other pile of inanimate objects.

God's question to Ezekiel was 'Can these bones live?' If he had asked me, I would probably have responded with a resounding no. Of course they can't live. They are long dead, they are damaged and dried, they are incomplete and muddled with each other, they have no capacity for life at all. Ezekiel, however, answered, 'Lord, you know'. He had faith: not in the miracle he didn't know he was about to witness, but faith that God wanted to show him something. He had faith that, while he didn't know the answer, God was about to make a point or do a work that would surprise him. God always did. Ezekiel's answer made no judgement on what he was seeing, but invited the next part of the learning process from a trusted teacher.

The last two images of restoration that we looked at were based in familiar processes, even if the outcome took those processes further than human experience. We are familiar with how silver is refined, even though the silver we end up with might not be entirely pure. We are familiar with how a ruined place can be rebuilt and a destroyed landscape can be replanted, even though when we do it ourselves it may not reach the heights of the garden of Eden. However, with this image God shows Ezekiel something that is not remotely possible within human skill. Even today, with all our medicine, advances in genetics and cures for devastating diseases, we cannot make dry bones come to life. We can't even stop them from dying in the first place. Only God can. In Ezekiel's vision, God lets us in to the secrets of a strange and wonderful process that we can only imagine.

In verse 11, the identity of the bones is made explicit: they represent the house of Israel. In captivity in Babylon at the time, the people had lost hope of ever returning home to become their own nation again. It seemed as unlikely as dry bones being brought to life. In this prophecy, God not only restores hope of a homecoming, but also gives a few details about how it will be achieved. First, the bones, like the scattered people and tribes, come together and are rejoined. Their strength is renewed with muscles and sinews, and they are clothed with flesh and skin. Breath, which is God's spirit, comes into them so that they can once again live and move as God's people. Then, says God, they will be placed on their own soil (v. 14). In the vision, Ezekiel is told to prophesy these different stages to the bones, just as his voice will talk Israel through the stages of their restoration to come.

Listening to God's instruction at every stage will be key to completing the process.

When things seem utterly hopeless, either for ourselves or for our world, we can take hope from Ezekiel's valley of bones; and not just because it offers an image of resurrection which we can recognise with post-New-Testament eyes. We learn from this vision that God does the impossible, and that he does so not always all at once, but sometimes with a process: step by step, with an end in mind. If we listen out for his voice, follow the instruction and take the next small step, we will eventually be restored. We may only be able to see one step ahead. Joining bones together into complete skeletons still doesn't make it look possible to bring them back to life, but it's one step closer to possible. Moving from despair to a little hope might be the first step towards experiencing a miracle.

A question

What is the first step towards your most impossible hope?

A prayer

Lord, can these bones live? You know. Please show me.

Friday

Joined together

The word of the Lord came to me: Mortal, take a stick and write on it, 'For Judah, and the Israelites associated with it'; then take another stick and write on it, 'For Joseph (the stick of Ephraim) and all the house of Israel associated with it'; and join them together into one stick, so that they may become one in your hand...

When the sticks on which you write are in your hand before their eyes, then say to them, Thus says the Lord God: I will take the people of Israel from the nations among which they have gone, and will gather them from every quarter, and bring them to their own land. I will make them one nation in the land, on the mountains of Israel; and one king shall be king over them all. Never again shall they be two nations, and never again shall they be divided into two kingdoms. They shall never again defile themselves with their idols and their detestable things, or with any of their transgressions. I will save them from all the apostasies into which they have fallen, and will cleanse them. Then they shall be my people, and I will be their God.

EZEKIEL 37:15–17, 20–23

Immediately after Ezekiel's experience in the valley of dry bones, these next instructions from God take the first part of the prophecy to the bones – the joining together – and expand it into a new prophecy for Israel.

I once read a sweet story about a couple who had been through a stressful time and were having lots of arguments. They tried not to shout at each other within earshot of the children, but they were not always successful. One day, their youngest child took two pieces of paper, wrote 'Mum' on one and 'Dad' on the other, stuck them together with sticky tape and left them on the kitchen table, the perfect toddler version of a prophetic action. That is more or less exactly what Ezekiel was asked to do in this passage. His action in joining the two sticks, one for Judah and one for Joseph, showed God's desire for the deeply divided nation of Israel to come together as one again. This would be their first step towards restoration as a nation, which would include God gathering his scattered people, ending their idolatry and bringing them into a land of their own.

The vision of the restored nation that follows is worth reading (Ezekiel 37:24–28). It is full of hints of Jesus, and although it refers to Israel it is clearly also a heavenly vision, a perfect time yet to come for the whole world. There will be one king, called a shepherd, king David, their prince forever; there will be an everlasting covenant of peace; God's dwelling place will be among his people. The prophecy that begins with the gathering up and joining together of the scattered people and tribes finishes with the joining of humanity and God, heaven and earth. Like Psalm 103, which we read in part two, this passage is cross-shaped, with the horizontal line of human unity matching the vertical line of God and humans reconciled. The restoration of all things seems to rely on these ingredients: forgiveness for sin, peace between people, peace between heaven and earth. It resonates with the song of the angels at Jesus' birth. It is a picture of the final result of the saving work of God.

In this restored nation, says God, the people will never again go back to their old ways, defiling themselves with idols. Instead, they will be united in the worship of their one God, who will be their God and they his people. Like the image of the purified silver in Malachi or the earlier image of Eden, this is a picture of a world from which sin has been not just forgiven, but entirely removed: they will be cleansed and never return to their transgressions.

In Romans 8, Paul writes about the 'before' picture to this prophecy, saying that the whole of creation is waiting – groaning, as if in labour – to be set free from the corruption caused by sin. Sin affects creation, and in this picture from Ezekiel it is the healing of the distance between people that is the beginning of setting creation free. From the wars between nations to the squabbles within families, the lack of peace in the world contributes to its fallen state, and we can see the truth of that all around us. When we talk about climate change, our dying oceans or the burning rainforests, perhaps we should also be talking about peace, because it is all connected. The world is waiting longingly and painfully for a restoration that begins with the joining together of its people in the worship of their God. We could make a start on that today.

A question

How can you make peace in your corner of the world?

A prayer

Father, I can see that everything – all of creation – is groaning and longing for peace. Help me to restore what I can, to reach out to who I can, to be careful with the parts of creation and the people you have given to me. Guide me in doing this as a tiny part of your great restoration. Amen

A new creation

For the love of Christ urges us on, because we are convinced that one has died for all; therefore all have died. And he died for all, so that those who live might live no longer for themselves, but for him who died and was raised for them.

From now on, therefore, we regard no one from a human point of view; even though we once knew Christ from a human point of view, we know him no longer in that way. So if anyone is in Christ, there is a new creation: everything old has passed away; see, everything has become new! All this is from God, who reconciled us to himself through Christ, and has given us the ministry of reconciliation; that is, in Christ God was reconciling the world to himself, not counting their trespasses against them, and entrusting the message of reconciliation to us. So we are ambassadors for Christ, since God is making his appeal through us; we entreat you on behalf of Christ, be reconciled to God.

2 CORINTHIANS 5:14–20

Have you ever discovered something extraordinary, something that will always make you look at the world in a slightly different way? I love the moment in one of my favourite films, *Amélie*, when Félix Lerbier learns that there are more potential connections in his brain than atoms in the universe. He looks up from his magazine, absolutely stunned, while the world continues turning as normal around him. I can think of a few moments in my own life which, to varying degrees, changed my outlook: some were big shifts, such as becoming a parent; others were smaller but still significant, such as visiting ancient Pompeii and realising how close in history we are to the time of the New Testament.

In this passage, Paul is writing to the church in Corinth and trying to explain how he and his fellow apostles have been changed by their encounter with Christ. Although everything about the world might look the same, he draws the attention of his readers to the event that has, in fact, changed everything. He says that at the moment Christ died, there was a monumental shift in reality which, once you have noticed it, will change your outlook on life forever.

Because Christ died for everyone, says Paul, everyone has died. There is an old era that has already ended, signalling a fundamental change for everybody in the world. Everybody now has the same chance of being raised to new life in Christ. In this new life, he explains, we no longer live selfishly, with ourselves as our goal, but we live for Christ. Our direction and purpose are different.

For Paul and the apostles and anyone who follows Jesus, life is lived differently, and so everything now looks different. Our outlook has been changed. We see Jesus, other people and the whole world with new eyes.

This is all possible, says Paul, because we are entirely new creations. Even though we have not yet reached God's new heaven and new earth, the end point of God's plan to restore the world, we are beginning that new life here and now, on earth the way it is.

So, we are new creations, living a new life in a changed reality, but surrounded by others who have not yet encountered it. That, says Paul, gives us a particular ministry. Paul uses the language of ambassadors, because as new creations on earth, we are citizens of a new kingdom, representatives of heaven. If nothing else changes the way we exist in the world, the word 'ambassadors' should. Do we live the way heavenly life could be lived? Are our priorities, our desires and our hopes those of heaven? Are we genuinely looking at the world with new eyes? As ambassadors of heaven, how can we open the eyes of those around us to this new kingdom and further the work of God in restoring his world? Paul argues that this is our new purpose: to invite others into this shifted reality that leads to reconciliation between heaven and earth.

In previous passages we have seen how this works: the cross-shaped peace, with the first step of reconciliation between people leading to eventual reconciliation between heaven and earth. In Paul's picture, though, God has reached out along the vertical line first, giving his people on earth the task of reaching out across the horizontal to gather everyone into his grace. The previous pictures gathered all the scattered tribes of Israel; Paul's picture includes not just Israel but all people, since Christ died for all. The visions and prophecies we saw in Ezekiel were of a perfect, finished world, a restored Eden: visions of heaven on earth at last. In Paul's picture, God's new creation begins within every follower of Jesus living a restored reality in Christ, sharing that reality with others, all the while looking forward to God's finished heavenly world.

A question

What would it look like for you to be an ambassador of heaven?

A prayer

Father, sometimes the tension of being a new creation in a fallen world is hard to bear. I get confused; I know I can't see the full picture and don't have all the answers, yet I am still your ambassador, and that responsibility feels huge sometimes. Guide me with your Spirit and fill me with the hope and the vision of your restored creation, so that I can invite others into this wonderful truth. Amen

End of section questions

- What would a perfect earth look like?
- What hints and hopes can you see of God's new creation – in the world and in other people?
- What has been destroyed, in your life or in the lives of people you know? What would it look like for those things to be restored?
- In what ways can we start to work towards a restored world now?
- How important is unity to God's restored world? What can we do about it?
- Have any of these images of restoration changed the way you see the world, others or yourself?

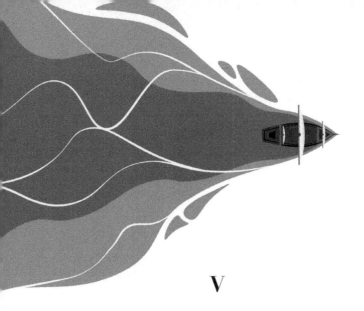

V

Images of reconciliation

We finished last week by considering Paul's words saying that we are 'ministers of reconciliation', reaching out to gather the world into peaceful relationship with God. We saw that the joining together of people was the first step towards the new heaven and new earth promised in so many visions and prophecies throughout the Bible.

This week we will look more closely at reconciliation, the peace between people which leads to peace between God and humanity. We will start with three stories of reconciliation. Two of them are stories of brothers from the book of Genesis. The third is the parable of the prodigal son, which we began in part one when we looked at images of repentance; we will read the end of that story on Tuesday.

Next, we will look at further scriptural images and metaphors for reconciliation, ways of thinking about what it means for the earth to be at peace and for heaven and earth to be at peace with one another, hunting for more echoes of Eden like the one we saw in Ezekiel 36. As we move onwards through this week towards Holy Week, we will find plenty of reminders of passages we have encountered earlier in this book. We are beginning to see God's peace-plan coming together and reaching a turning point for the world.

Jacob and Esau

Now Jacob looked up and saw Esau coming, and four hundred men with him. So he divided the children among Leah and Rachel and the two maids. He put the maids with their children in front, then Leah with her children, and Rachel and Joseph last of all. He himself went on ahead of them, bowing himself to the ground seven times, until he came near his brother.

But Esau ran to meet him, and embraced him, and fell on his neck and kissed him, and they wept. When Esau looked up and saw the women and children, he said, 'Who are these with you?' Jacob said, 'The children whom God has graciously given your servant.' Then the maids drew near, they and their children, and bowed down; Leah likewise and her children drew near and bowed down; and finally Joseph and Rachel drew near, and they bowed down. Esau said, 'What do you mean by all this company that I met?' Jacob answered, 'To find favour with my lord.' But Esau said, 'I have enough, my brother; keep what you have for yourself.'

GENESIS 33:1–9

Jacob was terrified. After 20 years away, he was heading back to face his older twin brother Esau, from whom he had fled all those years ago. He had tricked Esau out of his birthright and tricked their father, Isaac, into blessing him instead of Esau. No wonder his brother had last been seen beside himself with anger, threatening to kill Jacob. Now, Jacob had heard that Esau was on his way to meet him, with 400 men.

Jacob began to organise his large household like a military operation. He divided them up into two separate travelling groups, so that if Esau attacked one of them, the other might escape. Then he took a vast quantity of his livestock – goats, sheep, camels, cows and donkeys – and sent them off ahead, bit by bit, with his servants. Each servant was charged with a message for Esau that these were gifts for him from Jacob, who was following behind. Perhaps so many gifts would mollify Esau, so that by the time Jacob and his family reached him, he would show them some mercy. In his messages, Jacob was careful to address Esau as 'My lord'. In fact, Isaac's blessing had made Jacob lord over Esau (see Genesis 27:37), but Jacob was more than willing to place himself humbly into Esau's hands if it might save his life.

This still wasn't enough for Jacob. He looked at his family – two wives, two maids, eleven sons so far and a daughter – and, with a similar inclination towards favouritism that had caused the rift between him and Esau in the first place, he divided them up as well, sending the maids with their children ahead of Leah with hers, and placing his favourite wife Rachel at the very back with her only son, little Joseph, the light of Jacob's life. They were in the most protected position. Everybody else would have to fall before they did.

Then, the night before they were to walk into Esau's territory, Jacob sent the rest of the camp on ahead, and he stayed and wrestled all night with a stranger who gave him a new name: Israel, which means 'One who strives with God'. The stranger blessed him, and Jacob declared that he had seen God face to face and yet survived.

The following day, after all that preparation, Esau 'ran to meet him, and fell on his neck and kissed him, and they wept' (v. 4) – a phrase which we will hear echoes of more than once this week. All was forgiven, the gifts unnecessary, the careful ordering of his family irrelevant, as Esau welcomed them all with joy.

It is not for nothing that the wrestling incident happened alongside this brotherly reunion. The all-night wrestling, and the new name of

Israel, was another symbol given by God: a real-life picture of the part future generations would play in reconciling earth and heaven. After all, where else have we seen a picture of somebody who has been wronged, running to meet a long-lost traveller on the road, a traveller who has decided to humble himself to the position of servant just in case?

Israel gave his new name to a nation who would continue to strive with God, to resist being at peace with God; but Jacob prevailed and received blessing, just as the people of Israel always hoped to do. Jacob's approach to Esau was so like the way in which the nation of Israel would often approach God in the future, fearing wrath rather than trusting mercy, trying to protect themselves rather than trusting God's promise of protection.

They are not the only ones. How often do we approach God the way Jacob approached Esau? We put our best efforts out in front, hoping that God will be won over by the gifts of our good works, while we hide the things he might be less pleased with or tuck our treasures away behind our backs in case God wants to take them from us. We might approach with trepidation, expecting anger and destruction. Of course, some of that is due to the messages we have heard from others. Some of us have been told that God is storming out to meet us with an army of 400 and a look of thunder on his face. But that is not true. When we pray like that, we haven't understood the character of God nor appreciated how safe we are in his hands and how eager he is to meet us with mercy, forgiveness and love.

A question

What have you heard about God? What is the look on his face as he runs to meet you?

A prayer

Father, sometimes I worry about what you'll say when you see me. I work out what to show you and what to hide, how best to appease you. Help me to remember that you are not like that. I want to bring everything I am and everything I have into your welcoming, open arms. Amen

Joseph and his brothers

Then Joseph said to his brothers, 'Come closer to me.' And they came closer. He said, 'I am your brother Joseph, whom you sold into Egypt. And now do not be distressed, or angry with yourselves, because you sold me here; for God sent me before you to preserve life. For the famine has been in the land these two years; and there are five more years in which there will be neither ploughing nor harvest. God sent me before you to preserve for you a remnant on earth, and to keep alive for you many survivors. So it was not you who sent me here, but God; he has made me a father to Pharaoh, and lord of all his house and ruler over all the land of Egypt. Hurry and go up to my father and say to him, "Thus says your son Joseph, God has made me lord of all Egypt; come down to me, do not delay…" And now your eyes and the eyes of my brother Benjamin see that it is my own mouth that speaks to you. You must tell my father how greatly I am honoured in Egypt, and all that you have seen. Hurry and bring my father down here.' Then he fell upon his brother Benjamin's neck and wept, while Benjamin wept upon his neck. And he kissed all his brothers and wept upon them; and after that his brothers talked with him.

GENESIS 45:4–9, 12–15

Jacob's favourite son, Joseph, the one who was tucked out of the way of the expected wrath of Esau, grew up to suffer from his brothers' jealousy. Hardly surprising, given Jacob's blatant favouritism for the firstborn of his favoured wife, Rachel. Joseph's brothers nearly killed him, but thanks to traders passing at the right moment, they sold him instead, sending him into slavery in Egypt. Thankfully, Joseph's faith and his knack for interpreting dreams meant that he ended up as second in command to Pharaoh, leading Egypt through the famine that he had accurately predicted, storing up enough food while the surrounding lands had nothing. So it was that his brothers, without recognising him, came begging for food, and the stage was set for their unlikely reunion.

In this passage, having persuaded them to fetch his youngest brother Benjamin, Joseph has finally decided to reveal his identity to his brothers. His words of forgiveness to them are remarkable: he has made his peace with what happened to him because of his clear insight that it was all intended by God to save, not just his brothers, but the whole nation of Egypt. The story of Joseph, like that of Jacob and Esau, is another one of God's real-life pictures, looking forward to Jesus. Joseph, the innocent party, accepted violence and estrangement from his brothers because to do so had preserved them – the twelve tribes of Israel – from a worse fate.

In forgiving his brothers, Joseph, who now holds all the power in this relationship, chooses to lay aside both his right and his ability to take revenge and instead opens the way to reconciliation. In Philippians, Paul says the same of Jesus, who 'did not regard equality with God as something to be exploited, but emptied himself, taking the form of a slave, being born in human likeness' and therefore was 'highly exalted' (Philippians 2:6–7, 9).

Their reconciliation does not return Joseph and his brothers to square one. Things don't go back to the way they were before, with Joseph at the bottom of the heap. Neither does Joseph's forgiveness leave his brothers grovelling. Instead, the brothers are invited into Joseph's new privileged position, so that all end up in a better place than they were before. Imagine a version of Cinderella in which, instead of punishing the ugly sisters and stepmother, Cinderella and Prince Charming invite them to rule with them from the palace. It's transformative forgiveness, which foresees how Jesus, by humbling himself, invites all people into the kingdom of heaven.

It's poignant that Joseph begins his speech with the words 'Come closer to me' (v. 4). Those words invite his brothers to cross a line behind which they have been fearfully trembling and to enter a place in which they will be given everything they have needed and more, through their brother's mercy. His next words, revealing his identity, will reunite and restore them. At last, he falls upon Benjamin's neck and weeps, in an echo of his father Jacob's encounter with Esau; he kisses all his brothers, and then they talk as equals.

The story of Joseph and his brothers offers us a picture that is simultaneously about reconciliation between God and people in Jesus and about how forgiveness can be possible between humans. Forgiveness between people is rarely seen in the Old Testament. Reconciliation was possible, but only God could truly forgive. Yet here we have an image of forgiveness: we see Joseph giving up his right to anger, bitterness and revenge in order to bless his brothers. It's a description of how forgiveness actually works: it's not merely a question of saying that everything is all right now, but it takes effort and sacrifice to make it really so. We can be challenged by the story of Joseph when it comes to our turn to forgive others, and it can also lead us into a greater understanding of the work of forgiveness and how Jesus has performed that work for us.

A question

Why is forgiveness so difficult and so rare?

A prayer

Lord, I see that forgiveness is a process, that it is difficult, that it involves humility and sacrifice. Thank you for taking on all of that for me. Help me to do the same when people have hurt me, all the while leaning on your strength.

Tuesday

_____

The other brother

'Now his elder son was in the field; and when he came and approached the house, he heard music and dancing... Then he became angry and refused to go in. His father came out and began to plead with him. But he answered his father, "Listen! For all these years I have been working like a slave for you, and I have never disobeyed your command; yet you have never given me even a young goat so that I might celebrate with my friends. But when this son of yours came back, who has devoured your property with prostitutes, you killed the fatted calf for him!" Then the father said to him, "Son, you are always with me, and all that is mine is yours. But we had to celebrate and rejoice, because this brother of yours was dead and has come to life; he was lost and has been found."'

LUKE 15:25, 28–32

Early in our marriage, my husband and I made an agreement that neither of us would leave and drive away in the middle of an argument: we promised that we would stay where we were and sort it out. Not long after that agreement, we had an enormous row about something – neither one of us can remember what it was – and my husband stormed out of the room and disappeared. Having called for him in the house and garden and received no reply, I was convinced that he had broken our vow, so I left the house and went looking for him on my motorbike, completely missing the fact that our car was still parked in the village car park that we used.

At the time, we lived in a tiny cottage with the kind of lock that needed a key to open the door whether you were inside or outside.

After fruitlessly roaming around the village and environs, I came back to the house to discover that not only had my husband not left, but I had locked him in! He had only been sitting in his study, taking deep breaths as he prepared for the next round of debate, when he heard the door slam. By the time I had returned, he was wondering whether he might need to climb out of a window. Thankfully, we were both too relieved – and too busy laughing at my extraordinary lack of observation – to continue the original fight any further.

You don't need to have gone very far to be in need of reconciliation. At the end of the parable of the prodigal son, the father has met his younger son on the road, rejoiced over him, brought him home and thrown a party. But the older son, who has been there all along, is left out in the cold. He feels angry because, from his point of view, this younger brother of his has behaved terribly and been rewarded for it, while he, the older brother, has remained dutiful and never received such a reward. His language to his father is telling: he has been working 'like a slave', he says, and never disobeyed (v. 29). The fact that he sees himself as enslaved and has never asked his father for anything, shows that he is just as distant from his father in attitude as his younger brother was in miles. He has not understood the character of his father any better than his brother has, because both of them have assumed that the father is not ready to give them anything: the younger brother thought he had to take what he wanted and run; the older simply resigned himself to a life of drudgery.

The younger brother realised his mistake, turned back towards home and found the father running down the road to greet him. In his reconciliation, he has learned that his father is loving and generous, always willing to give. We do not know the ending of the story for the older brother. I wonder how he took his father's words, 'You are always with me, and all that is mine is yours' (v. 31)? Did he believe them, and realise that he, too, had made a mistake and needed to reconcile himself to his father as well as to his brother? Or did he shake his head bitterly, feeling that in his experience those words were just not true?

Of course, the answer is neither, because the older brother is fictional. Jesus didn't finish his story, because the ending of the parable was a challenge to all the older brothers in his audience. Right back at the beginning of chapter 15, we see that all the 'tax-collectors and sinners' had come to listen to Jesus (v. 1), but they had been joined by the Pharisees and scribes, who were grumbling about the company Jesus kept. Jesus was telling this parable to a mixed group of younger and older brothers, but it was the grumbling listeners who were left with a choice. Do you feel that you have always been in the father's house, but never celebrated? That you have followed all God's commandments to the letter until it felt like drudgery, but never seen a result? If God told you that you have always been with him, but it is right to celebrate when a long-lost sinner takes a step towards home, how would you react?

In the end, the story of the prodigal son is another cross-shaped passage. For everyone to be reconciled to God, humans also need to find peace with one another. Brothers need to welcome long-lost brothers to be part of the household of God; otherwise, they will be left out in the cold.

We don't need to have gone very far to be in need of reconciliation. Some of us are still standing outside the party, feeling hard done by, not understanding that God has never loved us for our efforts or obedience, but as his children. Why don't we go in, and be a part of the celebration?

A question

Who would be the hardest for you to welcome? What can you do to change that?

A prayer

Dear Father, please forgive me when I find it hard to imagine certain people being welcomed and celebrated in your house. When someone turns to you, whoever they are and whatever they have done, may my reaction be only rejoicing.

Near and far off

But now in Christ Jesus you who once were far off have been brought near by the blood of Christ. For he is our peace; in his flesh he has made both groups into one and has broken down the dividing wall, that is, the hostility between us. He has abolished the law with its commandments and ordinances, so that he might create in himself one new humanity in place of the two, thus making peace, and might reconcile both groups to God in one body through the cross, thus putting to death that hostility through it. So he came and proclaimed peace to you who were far off and peace to those who were near; for through him both of us have access in one Spirit to the Father. So then you are no longer strangers and aliens, but you are citizens with the saints and also members of the household of God, built upon the foundation of the apostles and prophets, with Christ Jesus himself as the cornerstone. In him the whole structure is joined together and grows into a holy temple in the Lord; in whom you also are built together spiritually into a dwelling-place for God.

EPHESIANS 2:13–22

Paul is writing to Gentiles (non-Jews) in this passage. Just before these verses, he reminds them that they were once strangers to Israel and to the covenants and promises of God, and that as such they had no hope. In Christ Jesus, though, those who 'once were far off have been brought near' (v. 13). I wonder whether Paul has the parable of the prodigal son in mind when he compares those who were 'far off' with those who were near. If so, he adds another layer of understanding to the parable by imagining the 'far off' as Gentiles, rather than the tax collectors and sinners in the crowd Jesus was addressing. It makes

Israel into the older son, the one who has always been near the Father, yet never quite reconciled.

Paul offers a further ending to the parable. We saw yesterday that the oldest son was left hanging at the end of the story: would he decide to go in to the party or not? Could he accept reconciliation with his younger brother? Paul states that the reconciliation has now happened through Christ, our peace. There is 'one new humanity in place of the two' (v. 15), and both groups are now, equally and together, reconciled to God through the cross.

This passage is full of pictures and metaphors as Paul explains the new state of peace that exists. First, he says that Christ has broken down a dividing wall, representing the hostility between Jews and Gentiles.

I have a slight memory of the fall of the Berlin Wall. I was only seven at the time, but I remember being called to watch the news and told that something momentous was happening. Much later, I visited Berlin and the museum at Checkpoint Charlie, learning about life while the wall was still in place and the astounding efforts that some had made to cross it, risking their lives and freedom in the process. Very few succeeded. I remember noting the differences that still existed in the infrastructure in what used to be East and West Berlin, and being surprised by the enormous impact a physical structure – representing so much more than its bricks and barbed wire – had made in the history of a city. Paul says that Christ's peace has healed a much deeper and longer division in humanity.

Hold on tight, because Paul now starts to jump between images like a frog hopping across lily pads. He moves on to talk about citizenship, saying that Gentiles, who used to be foreigners, are now equal citizens in the same kingdom as Israel. In a leap of metaphor, he identifies that kingdom as God's household: a family together, under one roof and with the same head. From there he makes another metaphorical frog-hop to imagining the house itself, a building into which both Gentile and Jewish stones are built on the foundation stones of the apostles and prophets, with Christ as the cornerstone, ordering everything. Another little jump and the house is a temple, allowing all these people, coming together peacefully, to create a dwelling place for God on earth.

Here, Paul lays out something that has been hinted at in many of the passages we have encountered so far in this book. He sees Christ at the centre of the shape of a cross: breaking down a dividing wall to bring Jews and Gentiles together into one holy people and reconciling both groups to God. Christ is our peace, both on earth, and between heaven and earth.

To achieve this, Christ is at the centre of every image. He is at the centre of the cross shape, breaking down the wall. He is the king of the one kingdom, the head of the household, the cornerstone of the building, which becomes the dwelling place of God. He is the one proclaiming peace to the ones who were far off and peace to the ones who were near. If we are looking for reconciliation, in any direction and at any distance, we need to turn to Christ, because stepping closer to the centre brings us closer, in the end, to everyone and everything.

A question

Who do you see as 'far off'?

A prayer

Lord, I was far off. Thank you for bringing me into your household, for fitting me into the stones of your temple. May I always have you at the centre of everything I think, say and do, and especially in my dealings with others, remembering that you are our peace.

Thursday

The wolf and the lamb

The wolf shall live with the lamb,
  the leopard shall lie down with the kid,
the calf and the lion and the fatling together,
  and a little child shall lead them.
The cow and the bear shall graze,
  their young shall lie down together;
  and the lion shall eat straw like the ox.
The nursing child shall play over the hole of the asp,
  and the weaned child shall put its hand on the adder's den.
They will not hurt or destroy
  on all my holy mountain;
for the earth will be full of the knowledge of the Lord
  as the waters cover the sea.

ISAIAH 11:6–9

A photograph of two elderly men smiling together in the sunshine on a railway bridge may, at first, look unremarkable. The story behind it, however, makes it as surprising and unlikely as a lion eating straw like an ox. The photograph is of Eric Lomax, who became a prisoner of war in Japan in 1942, standing next to Nagase Takashi, his torturer, at the Burma railway, which Lomax had been forced to construct in appalling conditions. In the prisoner-of-war camp, Lomax had managed to build a small radio, and, when it was discovered, Nagase had interrogated him and overseen his torture, using his role as interpreter for cruel taunts. When the two men met in 1998, Lomax imagined that he would somehow take revenge for his broken bones and psychological torment. Instead, when Nagase approached him weeping and apologising, they became good friends and continued to meet up over the next 18 years until Nagase's death, even drawing on the past experiences they had in common to build their friendship.

In this passage from Isaiah, the prophet presents a vision of friendship between sworn enemies. Predators live with their prey in peace, lying down next to them, eating grass and straw instead of the flesh of their new friends. Layered in among these images of unimaginable peace are some important symbols.

Isaiah 11 is a messianic prophecy, beginning with the new shoot that will grow from the cut-off stump of Jesse. Isaiah is describing the reign of this new prince, who judges so righteously that perfect peace ensues. In the picture of a little child leading all these animals, then, perhaps we have an image of the Christ child, a hint of the incarnation that will mean God existing as a small child on earth. Even more significantly, the child in this passage plays over the hole of the asp and covers the adder's den with his hand. This child is the answer to the curse to the serpent in Genesis 3:15: 'I will put enmity between you and the woman, and between your offspring and hers; he will strike your head, and you will strike his heel.' There is, though, no violence to the snake in this image, no continued enmity. Instead, the serpent stays in its hole and does not harm the child. The child's hand over the adder's den prevents the snake from coming out to disturb the peace: it is being kept in its place.

The image culminates with the beautiful lines: 'For the earth will be full of the knowledge of the Lord as the waters cover the sea' (v. 9). Just as we saw in yesterday's passage that Christ was at the centre of everything and making peace possible, here we see that the reason for the success of this peaceful existence is that the whole world knows God, intimately and thoroughly, as the waters cover the sea: in other words, so completely that the two are indistinguishable and impossible to separate.

These passages all come with a challenge, though. It's the challenge to the older brother, the challenge to the Jew and to the Gentile, the challenge to the wolf and to the lamb: now that reconciliation has been made possible, can you agree to it? Can you go through with it? And in this example, reconciliation is a more costly prospect to the lamb than it is to the wolf. The little child leading them must have a remarkably reassuring presence.

This picture of peaceful creation has no human being in it, apart from the child. Can we imagine ourselves as part of it? Perhaps we can, but only if we fully appreciate what it would look like in human terms. The murderer shall live with the victim; the abuser shall lie down with the abused; the torturer and his prisoner shall go on holiday together, and a little child shall lead them. Can we stomach it? Is it still such a beautiful image? Looking back at the photograph of Eric Lomax and Nagase Takashi, I think it is; but it's no wonder that the earth will need to be filled with the knowledge of God for it to become a reality.

A question

What would proper peace actually look like – globally, and in your own life?

A prayer

Come, Lord Jesus, and lead us into peace.

Face to face

Love never ends. But as for prophecies, they will come to an end; as for tongues, they will cease; as for knowledge, it will come to an end. For we know only in part, and we prophesy only in part; but when the complete comes, the partial will come to an end. When I was a child, I spoke like a child, I thought like a child, I reasoned like a child; when I became an adult, I put an end to childish ways. For now we see in a mirror, dimly, but then we will see face to face. Now I know only in part; then I will know fully, even as I have been fully known.
1 CORINTHIANS 13:8–12

I don't know what I did to deserve a brass player in the family, but my son has been learning the trombone for several years now. He has moved beyond the stage of merely making rude noises and is learning some good tunes that leave the whole family with earworms after every practice. A cellist myself, I think that the trombone must be the most fiendishly difficult instrument ever devised. To find a note, the slide must be taken to one of seven different unmarked positions – sitting just outside one of them will make the note out of tune – and then within each one of those positions, there are at least three or four different possible notes, depending on the speed at which the player vibrates their lips against the mouthpiece. My son's arms are still too short to reach the furthest position. To play a piece of music, he has to look at each note on the page, decide what it is, remember which position it's in and then hope to select the right embouchure for it, and have a good enough ear to decide whether what comes out is correct. No wonder he thinks he will never learn to sight-read in time for his exam.

And yet, I know – and I keep trying to tell him – that one day, he will not have to go through all those steps. Every musician, no matter what their instrument, reaches a stage where their eyes see the note and they immediately play it, without thinking, without needing to consciously name the note or find a position. They just know. It's as easy as reading fluently, driving a car or anything else that is very difficult when you begin and becomes second nature.

Yesterday's passage from Isaiah finished with the thought that, when all creation is at peace, the world will be filled with the knowledge of God 'as the waters cover the sea' (Isaiah 11:9). Today, we have Paul's description of that same moment, from his letter to the church in Corinth. When complete and full knowledge of God comes, he says, there will be no more need for any of the things that only hint of God's glory. He explains it in terms of being a child and being an adult: at some point, your reasoning and behaviour have changed sufficiently that you have grown up and you see the world in a different way. There will be no more need for prophecy or tongues or any of the things that take us towards God in little steps, because we will just know.

What will it be like to know God so completely? Paul offers another image. He says that now, we are looking into a mirror 'dimly' (v. 12). The Greek word translated 'dimly' also means 'riddle', the same word from which we get 'enigma'. Mirrors of the ancient world would not have shown the clear reflections we know today. Paul means something more like looking at yourself in the back of a spoon – the reflection is hazy, distorted, unreliable. It is a riddle, something you have to guess at and work out step by step.

But one day, we will see God 'face to face'. This image is not just about being able to see God clearly, but it is about being able to withstand the gaze of God. It recalls the story of Moses up the mountain, allowed to see God retreating as he passed, but not the full force of his face; or the story of Moses having to veil his own face after encountering God because it was shining. Humans have never been able to come face to face with the full glory of God.

However, it is also a tender image. It calls to mind two lovers or a parent gazing into the face of a newborn child. The phrase itself, even the words on the page, looks like a reflection: two faces, facing each other.

Paul has another way to explain it. He says that one day he will know fully, even as he has been fully known. If you have a moment, read Psalm 139 and think about how fully known you are by God. One day we will know God with the kind of complete, intimate knowledge that God has always known us. It won't take any effort, any study, any calculations; we will just *know*.

The beauty of this passage is that it is full of all the metaphors and explanations that will no longer be needed when we reach this full understanding and see God face to face. We won't need images of mirrors, children or enigmas, explaining the inexplicable. We won't need Paul. We won't need books like this one. We won't need metaphors at all. We will be face to face with the real thing.

A question

What is your most intimate relationship?

A prayer

Great, unknowable God, I love so many of the things I have learnt about you. Other things puzzle me, worry me or are simply too big for me to grasp. The idea that I will, one day, know you completely is astonishing. Thank you for making it possible, and, until that day, please add to my understanding and make me ready to see you face to face.

The temple curtain

Then Jesus gave a loud cry and breathed his last. And the curtain of the temple was torn in two, from top to bottom. Now when the centurion, who stood facing him, saw that in this way he breathed his last, he said, 'Truly this man was God's Son!'

MARK 15:37–39

I hadn't been quite sure that my children were ready for their first trip to a theatre, but when we saw that the presenters of their favourite television show were doing a tour, we decided we had to give it a go. Settling into our seats, I cast an anxious glance at my daughter, who sometimes struggled in unfamiliar places. I noted the confusion on her face. The curtains were closed across the stage, so the set wasn't visible. Had she understood my explanations of what we were doing there? Would she panic when the lights went down?

I needn't have worried. The show, carefully designed for small children, had a gentle start. One of the presenters came out in front of the stage, welcomed everybody, then stepped through the curtain as it opened on the familiar world of the television show. Both children were enthralled for an hour as they watched the world they had only ever seen on a screen break through into real life.

At the moment of Jesus' death, the massive curtain that hung in the temple, separating the holy of holies from the holy place, was torn in two from top to bottom. This was not a coincidence or a side effect of the earthquakes that were reported at the time. It was a powerful symbol of what had just happened. Jesus' death had opened the way for humans to approach God. No longer would a high priest need to make the terrifying trip behind the curtain, representing his people and atoning for their sins. Jesus himself had gone through that curtain and left it open. The ripped curtain revealed what had happened to Jesus: he had stepped into the presence of God, the holy of holies, not on earth in the temple, but in heaven. Now he had taken the place of the high priest, ministering in heaven on behalf of all humanity.

Just like the actor who stepped through the curtain as it opened, Jesus invited human beings into a world we had only ever known about at a distance. Visions we had seen in prophecies took on a new reality, like television characters turning out to be real people and appearing, large as life, in the room. The curtain in the temple was not the only thing that gave way when Jesus died. Think of all the barriers we have seen in the images that we explored this week: the fear of retaliation from a brother; the fear and destruction between predator and prey; the dividing wall of hostility between Jews and Gentiles; the veil that covered Moses' shining face; the mirror that distorts a reflection. The death of Jesus broke through them all.

It's strange that something being torn into two pieces should become the perfect symbol of everything being joined together. Or perhaps it is not strange, when we consider how destructive the crucifixion looks on the surface compared with what is happening underneath. Next week, we will travel together through the pain, darkness and violence of Holy Week, the events that took place leading up to Jesus' death on the cross. The temple curtain is a good reminder to carry with us, to show us that all may not be as it seems at first glance. By Easter morning, we will see how brokenness can be transformed, how an empty space can become a doorway.

Jesus made the way for us to have every kind of reconciliation, on earth and in heaven, because he went through first. When he died, he ripped a hole in the barrier between heaven and earth, and left it open. When he rose again, he ripped a hole in the barrier between death and life, and left it open. In forgiving the world, he made it possible for us to forgive each other. The way to peace and reconciliation may feel narrow sometimes, but it is open, and we can follow Jesus through.

A question

Where has Jesus made a way for you? What is on the other side?

A prayer

Loving Lord, you have opened up heaven and earth, and invited me into a new reality with you. Show me where you have made spaces for your peace to break through.

End of section questions

- Where are the dividing lines and walls in our communities? What happens when we try to reach across them?
- When does the church get involved with works of reconciliation? What more could be done?
- Who are the people we see as 'far off' or outsiders, and what are we doing to bring them closer?
- When have you felt like an outsider? What helped, or would have helped?
- How do you feel about the idea that there is a barrier between God and human beings which needs to be broken?

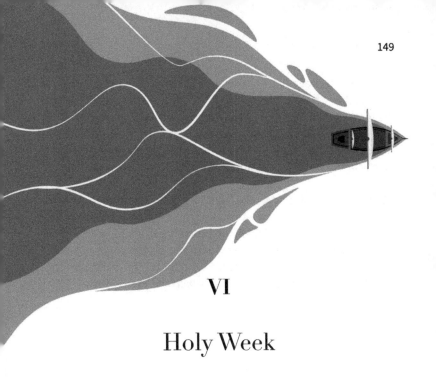

VI

Holy Week

Now we enter Holy Week and prepare to journey once again through the familiar events that take us from Palm Sunday to Easter Day: the last week of Jesus' life on earth. For anybody who has been here before, who is used to the church's pattern of seasons and the shape of Lent and Easter, Holy Week has its own expected rhythm and well-remembered texts, especially in the second half of the week.

However, perhaps this year, having looked closely at some of the images of sin and forgiveness and how they appear across the whole Bible, we might see more clearly how Holy Week plays out on a cosmic scale, forever changing heaven and earth.

As we watch the human events taking place this week, we can see God's plan of salvation: a plan that stretches back through history and reaches forward into eternity, one that gathers all people together across the earth and links them into heaven.

Some of the images we have seen will be specifically called to mind this week, as Jesus shares the Passover meal with his disciples and as he washes their feet. The timing of the crucifixion is surely a deliberate echo from God of those first Passover lambs. Perhaps this time, though, we might notice other echoes, other images and stories that speak about this ultimate story.

We will never fully understand the work that Jesus did on the cross until that moment when we finally stop seeing 'in a mirror, like a riddle' (see p. 143). Until then, all these images, metaphors and stories can help us: we discover ever more angles from which to see and comprehend the incomprehensible truth that Jesus really did die for us and that, somehow, this means we will have eternal life.

Palm Sunday

The donkey

Rejoice greatly, O daughter Zion!
   Shout aloud, O daughter Jerusalem!
Lo, your king comes to you;
   triumphant and victorious is he,
humble and riding on a donkey,
   on a colt, the foal of a donkey.
He will cut off the chariot from Ephraim
   and the warhorse from Jerusalem;
and the battle-bow shall be cut off,
   and he shall command peace to the nations;
his dominion shall be from sea to sea,
   and from the River to the ends of the earth.

ZECHARIAH 9:9–10

Throughout history, there have been all sorts of methods employed in making the sight and sound of an advancing army as terrifying as possible to the enemy. Perhaps the most ancient is the battle cry. According to Tacitus, Roman soldiers would put their shields in front of their mouths to amplify their battle cry, making it echo and resound. Musical instruments have the same effect across a distance, from the unstoppable onslaught of marching drums to the inexplicable (to the enemy) noise of the bagpipes.

Once the army is close enough to be seen, the sight has to match the sound. Native American warpaint, as well as communicating the roles and stations of the fighters, served to intimidate any opposing army. There was even warpaint for the horses. Genghis Khan brought extra horses into battle, either ridden by prisoners or with dummies mounted on them, to make the army appear larger – and at night, every soldier was commanded to light five campfires.

It's an understandable tactic which continues into the modern day with the stockpiling of nuclear weapons. Even the phrase 'sabre-rattling' to describe such behaviour must have its roots in exactly that threat of military might.

Jesus rode into Jerusalem on Palm Sunday, and the crowd waiting for him hailed him as the Son of David, the Messiah. Were they expecting a military leader, someone who would free them from Roman occupation? The palms they waved had once been a symbol of the flourishing of Israel, carved on the walls of the temple and stamped on their coins, and they cried 'Hosanna!', which means 'Save us!'

Jesus rode in without weapons, without warpaint, without drums or trumpets or a battle cry. He rode with his toes trailing the ground either side of a donkey. This was God riding into a holy city, God riding through a crowd of misled and sinful people, but there was no sabre-rattling, no display of might or threat of vengeance. He came in peace.

In choosing a donkey for his entrance to Jerusalem, Jesus was echoing this prophecy from Zechariah of a coming king. This king arrives victorious, riding a donkey because the battle has already been won. There is no need for a warhorse or a chariot, because he has brought peace. In fact, his whole purpose is peace: the king in this prophecy intends to cut off the warhorse and the battle bow, and command peace to the nations over the whole earth.

The people were shouting 'Hosanna! Save us!' and Jesus intended to save them. He had one battle left to fight, but rather than leading anybody else into battle behind him, he was heading to fight it alone, on their behalf. Once he emerged victorious, his only purpose would be peace: peace between the nations, and peace between heaven and earth.

Palm Sunday begins Holy Week with a picture of the God who could destroy, who holds the power and the right for justice, choosing to arrive in peace and offer forgiveness. Our victorious king can promise us peace because of his own victory against all the forces that were causing earth's war with heaven. Jesus riding into the final week of his life on a donkey is a perfect image of God's mercy.

The purpose of the king on the donkey is peace. He has come to command peace, to take away our weapons. Instead of palms, can we lay down our rattling sabres, our battle cries, all the things we hide behind to make ourselves look bigger than our enemies? Can we lay down our pride and cutting words and grudges, and ride onwards with him into real peace?

A question

What weapons do you wield?

A prayer

Hosanna, Son of David! Lord, save us! Praise to you, victorious king, whose purpose is peace forever!

Monday

The cleansing of the temple

Then Jesus entered the temple and drove out all who were
selling and buying in the temple, and he overturned the tables
of the money-changers and the seats of those who sold doves.
He said to them, 'It is written,

"My house shall be called a house of prayer";

but you are making it a den of robbers.'

The blind and the lame came to him in the temple, and he
cured them. But when the chief priests and the scribes saw
the amazing things that he did, and heard the children crying
out in the temple, 'Hosanna to the Son of David', they became
angry and said to him, 'Do you hear what these are saying?'
Jesus said to them, 'Yes; have you never read,

"Out of the mouths of infants and nursing babies

you have prepared praise for yourself"?'

MATTHEW 21:12–16

In an abrupt switch of images, we follow Jesus from his peaceful
entry into Jerusalem to his marching into the temple and overturning
tables. The God of peace angrily drives people out of his temple in a
mess of shouting, crashing and the flying feathers of frightened doves.
What is going on?

Occasionally, to inspire me to clean my own house, I watch one of
those programmes where a team of cleaners go into an obscenely
filthy or hoarded home and attempt to restore it to order before it is
condemned. Often the kitchen is the worst area of the house to be
tackled. You couldn't possibly prepare food or eat in it without getting several kinds of food poisoning. The fridge is full of mouldy food,
the cupboards are a haven for rats, mice and cockroaches, and flies

are breeding in the sink full of dirty dishes. Before any kind of deep cleaning can be done, the whole place has to be emptied, and most importantly, the vermin have to be evicted.

Jesus marched into the temple and swept out everything that didn't belong there. As a twelve-year-old, he had referred to the temple as 'my Father's house' (Luke 2:49); now, it must have seemed like coming home to a house full of squatters who had wrecked the place. The money changers were intruders, making an immoral fortune out of God's people who were trying to follow God's commands; they changed money for temple coins at unfavourable rates and sold sacrificial animals for far more than they were worth, so that people who had travelled too far to bring their own animals had to pay over the odds. It was as if, arriving at church, you had to rent a pew (extra for a cushion if you want to be comfy, and a blanket if you're cold), pay per hymn to be allowed to sing out loud and buy your wafer if you wanted to partake in Communion. In this way, the people buying and selling in the temple were putting barriers between people and the worship of God.

With these people still in place, the temple couldn't be used properly for its purpose. It was like a kitchen full of mould and rats, in which any food produced would be tainted: the worship of God was being tainted. Jesus cleared out the intruders, restoring the temple to its proper use, and then went straight into using it for God's glory. Once the kitchen is clean, the food that comes out of it is good again. Jesus spent his time in the temple revealing God's goodness, healing those who came to him there, while the voices of children praised him.

The chief priests and scribes were angry, because the children were naming Jesus as the Messiah (Son of David) and they expected him to silence them. This is the moment, in the gospel of Luke, when Jesus responds that if these voices were silenced, the rocks would cry out (Luke 19:39–40). The uncertainty about Jesus' identity, the way he used to warn insightful followers not to share that he was the Messiah, has ended. The veil is being lifted, the glass becoming clearer. The children's voices signify the removal of yet another barrier of understanding between God and his people; like dominoes, more will come tumbling down this week. For now, the Messiah was openly in God's purified temple, doing God's work and receiving worship.

The cleansing of the temple recalls some of the other images of cleaning that we have seen in this book. Do you remember in Isaiah 1 (part two) how bloodstains needed to be removed from the hands that were raised in worship? Or in Malachi (part four) how Judah and Jerusalem were purified like silver in order to stand before the Lord? This was the work Jesus was doing in the temple. He was removing the stain so that people could worship God; removing the dross so that the works of God for his people could shine through. It was only the beginning of the same work he would complete by the end of that week.

A question

If we are living stones being built into God's temple, what needs to be removed from us to allow for pure worship to take place?

A prayer

Lord Jesus, you sweep away injustice; your anger burns against those who put up barriers between God and the worship of his people. Where space has been made for you, wonderful things happen. Show me what thoughts need to be overturned in me, what attitudes need to be kicked out of me, for God's good works to take place in me. Amen

Tuesday

Authority to forgive

In the morning as they passed by, they saw the fig tree withered away to its roots. Then Peter remembered and said to
him, 'Rabbi, look! The fig tree that you cursed has withered.'
Jesus answered them, 'Have faith in God. Truly I tell you, if you
say to this mountain, "Be taken up and thrown into the sea",
and if you do not doubt in your heart, but believe that what
you say will come to pass, it will be done for you. So I tell you,
whatever you ask for in prayer, believe that you have received
it, and it will be yours.

'Whenever you stand praying, forgive, if you have anything
against anyone; so that your Father in heaven may also forgive
you your trespasses.'

Again they came to Jerusalem. As he was walking in the
temple, the chief priests, the scribes, and the elders came to
him and said, 'By what authority are you doing these things?
Who gave you this authority to do them?'

MARK 11:20–28

Have you ever read the whole Old Testament book of Esther right
through, like a novel? I recommend it; it's a great page-turner. Esther,
forced into marriage with a foreign king, finds that she is the only person who can save her whole people from her own husband – or rather,
from his evil adviser Haman, who has slyly persuaded the king to order
the destruction of the Jews. At the end of the story, once the villain
has been unveiled and dispatched, the king hands over his royal seal
to Esther, allowing her personally to draft the wording of the decree
that will save her people and to seal it in his name. It's a story that
plays with ideas of authority, from the reason King Xerxes needed a
new wife in the first place (his wife Vashti refused to acknowledge his

authority in front of their guests) to Haman hiding his own evil deeds under the king's authority, and then the king willingly handing his authority over to Esther.

In this passage from Mark, which takes place on the day after the cleansing of the temple in Holy Week, we witness an extraordinary shift in authority, but it all takes place in a series of strange snapshots, making it easy to miss. The disciples and Jesus are walking back into Jerusalem when they pass a fig tree. The day before, Jesus had cursed the same fig tree as they passed it, and now it has withered. They point this out, and Jesus responds by talking about mountains throwing themselves into the sea and forgiveness. Why?

Many of the moments in which the followers of Jesus had been convinced that he was more than just a teacher had to do with his power over the natural world. Peter had fallen to his knees in the boat after the miracle of the great catch of fish; the disciples had marvelled at Jesus' authority over the wind and waves when he calmed the storm. These seemed to be clues about the very nature and identity of Jesus, hints that in fact he had the power of God. The astonishment that met these feats was matched only by the astonishment that was voiced every time Jesus said that someone's sins had been forgiven. Only God could do that.

Here, though, when the disciples point out the withered fig tree, Jesus remarks that they, too, could have the same power over the natural world. With faith, he says, they could tell a mountain to be thrown into the sea and it would happen. The source of his power – an unbroken connection with God the Father – could be theirs as well, through prayer.

Then, seamlessly, he moves on to forgiveness, the other famous ability that had always shown that Jesus acted with the authority of God. He tells his disciples to forgive whoever has wronged them, whenever they are praying, so that their own sins will be forgiven. He moves forgiveness from something only God can do to something that his disciples not only can do, but are instructed to do, as part of their regular prayers. Jesus had taught them to say it the other way around before – 'Forgive us our sins, as we forgive others' – but here he tells them to begin with forgiveness. In John 20:23, after his resurrection, Jesus is even more specific about this new authority.

It makes sense that, in his gospel, Mark turns next to the moment when the scribes, elders and chief priests ask questions about Jesus' authority. Jesus has just been explaining to his disciples that the very same authority, which came from God to God's Son, would be passed to his followers like a royal seal, so that forgiveness – just as unlikely a feat as moving a mountain – would be part of their capability and responsibility.

We have visited the parable of the prodigal son a couple of times in this book already. Have you noticed that, at the moment of clothing his younger son, the father places a ring on his finger? Perhaps it is a signet ring; because our being forgiven restores us to our place in God's family so that we, too, have the authority to forgive. With great authority comes great responsibility, to misquote the ancient adage. Are we up to the task of forgiving our sisters and brothers so that they, too, can become a part of the family?

A question

Which is easier – to tell a mountain to jump into the sea or to forgive?

A prayer

Lord Jesus, you have made it clear time and time again that God's forgiveness for us and our forgiveness for others are inextricably wrapped up together. Help me to reach out to others just as you have reached out to me. I will need a faith that moves mountains to do it, but you have told me that it's possible. Amen

Pieces of silver

> Then Satan entered into Judas called Iscariot, who was one of the twelve; he went away and conferred with the chief priests and officers of the temple police about how he might betray him to them. They were greatly pleased and agreed to give him money. So he consented and began to look for an opportunity to betray him to them when no crowd was present.
>
> LUKE 22:3–6

Judas Iscariot knew the value of things. We know from John 12:6 that he acted as the treasurer for the disciples, but also that he helped himself to the money they had collected. That is the reason given for his reaction to the woman who poured expensive ointment over Jesus' feet: 'Why was this perfume not sold for three hundred denarii and the money given to the poor?' (John 12:5). In that story, Judas comes across as cynical and exacting: he knows how to estimate the value of the perfume accurately, but fails to estimate the value of the woman or the meaning of her gift. Meanwhile, the woman shows Jesus how much he is worth to her with the generous outpouring of such an expensive gift.

Similarly, in today's text, Judas weighs up what Jesus is worth to him. The gospel of Matthew tells us that the price paid was 30 pieces of silver, and it is difficult to work out how much that would be worth today due to not knowing how much each piece weighed and whether or not they were Roman coins. But, whichever way you look at it, it doesn't come out to a huge amount. In fact, it is less than the value Judas estimated for the woman's perfume.

It's interesting that 30 pieces of silver is the same price as the one required in Exodus 21:32 to compensate a slave owner for the accidental death of their slave. In other words, it is the rough cost of replacing a human being when the one you own can't work anymore. It's a mercenary, nominal fee that overlooks their worth as a person and redefines them as a tool.

Just as Judas had overlooked the woman and focused on the cost of her ointment, so he overlooks Jesus and instead thinks about what he can be used for and whether or not he has delivered what he promised. To Judas, the answer is no. Jesus has not started an uprising, nor made money amounting to the potential of his powers, nor defeated the Romans. Whatever Judas was expecting of Jesus, he has been disappointed. Jesus has no further use for him beyond 30 pieces of silver.

Do you find it difficult to imagine that anybody today could be so avaricious as Judas to think of people in terms of their monetary worth? Governments do this all the time. When they make decisions about which refugees can come from which country and how long they can stay, the decision is too often affected by whether these people will be able to work and pay taxes or will instead need support. In this country, disabled people are made to prove, over and over again, that they really cannot work before they can claim the benefits they need to survive. The comments on social media beneath any article about the need for food banks are enough to prove that plenty of people still think exactly like Judas. In fact, every time we judge the worth and dignity of a human being based on what they can give back to society, we are at risk of thinking in terms of those 30 pieces of silver.

Yet, even as Judas was valuing Jesus at the basic price of a human being, Jesus was valuing Judas – and each of us – at the heavenly price of a human being, which is absolutely everything. He knowingly allowed Judas to betray him so that he could pay that price with his life, letting all of us know our true worth in the eyes of the God who loves us.

A question

Where do we need to challenge society's views on the value of human beings?

A prayer

Lord Jesus, to you everyone is worth the same price: however old we are, wherever we're from, whatever our abilities are and no matter what we have done, we are each worth everything to you. Help me to see that value both in myself and in every person I meet. Amen

Maundy Thursday

Foot washing

And during supper Jesus, knowing that the Father had given all things into his hands, and that he had come from God and was going to God, got up from the table, took off his outer robe, and tied a towel around himself. Then he poured water into a basin and began to wash the disciples' feet and to wipe them with the towel that was tied around him. He came to Simon Peter, who said to him, 'Lord, are you going to wash my feet?' Jesus answered, 'You do not know now what I am doing, but later you will understand.' Peter said to him, 'You will never wash my feet.' Jesus answered, 'Unless I wash you, you have no share with me.' Simon Peter said to him, 'Lord, not my feet only but also my hands and my head!' Jesus said to him, 'One who has bathed does not need to wash, except for the feet, but is entirely clean. And you are clean, though not all of you.' For he knew who was to betray him; for this reason he said, 'Not all of you are clean.'

JOHN 13:2–11

Have you ever eaten in one of those establishments that is expensive enough for the waiting staff to place your napkin on your lap for you? It has only happened to me a couple of times, and I'm glad they are trained to work at lightning speed, otherwise I'm sure I would embarrass myself by reaching for the napkin first. It feels odd to have someone perform such a simple and intimate gesture. Much nicer was the experience I had when my sister treated me to a night out in Brussels at a seafood restaurant. After enjoying their signature meal of mussels, hot lemon towels were brought to banish the smell of fish from our hands and faces – sensory bliss.

For the disciples, foot washing must have been a combination of the two experiences. It was a common, necessary and relaxing sensation after a long dusty walk in sandals, but also an intimate task for even a slave or servant to perform. When it was their master and teacher with the towel around his waist, it felt much more awkward. Peter's reaction was understandable.

In telling the story, John makes a point of outlining who Jesus was before he describes him washing his disciples' feet. John draws attention to the remarkable contrast: Jesus, who had been given all things by God, chose to perform this servant's task. John also describes Jesus as being in a liminal moment: knowing that he had come from God and was going to God. The actions that take place in this last night of Jesus' earthly life become heavy with significance, and they begin with this act of service.

There is an echo here of a story we looked at last week. Jesus, kneeling before each disciple in turn to wash their feet, is like Joseph, choosing to reconcile with his eleven brothers instead of using the power he has to take revenge. Joseph and Jesus each demonstrate a deliberate choice to lay aside both power and the right they have to exercise that power, and instead place themselves back into a position of service, into the hands of those who hurt them. Jesus washed Judas' feet even though he knew who would betray him.

In fact, John frames the whole scene in what Jesus knows. He knows that the Father has given all things into his hands; he knows that he is going back to God; he knows who will betray him. With all of this knowledge, because of all of this knowledge, he kneels and washes his disciples' feet.

Many of us will have been to Maundy Thursday services today. Perhaps you have even allowed somebody to wash your feet or watched rather gratefully from the sidelines as it happens to someone else. We get over our feelings of awkwardness to allow ourselves to be served by others, as the disciples did. But how do we feel about allowing God to serve us? That is what the foot washing means. That was what Jesus was asking us to do.

But that is not all; there is a second part to Jesus' instruction. He tells his disciples that they must also wash one another's feet. He asks them to understand: 'Do you know what I have done to you?' (v. 12).

The challenge that Jesus gives us to wash one another's feet is not just a request for us to look after each other or even just a reminder that leaders should be servants too. It's a challenge to do what Joseph and Jesus both did: to choose to lay aside our right for revenge and serve even those who hurt us. And it's a challenge that increases the more power we have and the more vengeance we're due. When we are in positions of power, in any relationship, we most need to remember our call to wash feet.

A question

Which of your relationships most needs some foot washing?

A prayer

Lord, when you knew that you had power over everything, and you knew that you would be betrayed, you chose to lay it all aside and wash people's feet. You have asked me to do the same. Give me the wisdom, the grace and the strength to obey. Amen

Jesus Barabbas

Then they all shouted out together, 'Away with this fellow! Release Barabbas for us!' (This was a man who had been put in prison for an insurrection that had taken place in the city, and for murder.) Pilate, wanting to release Jesus, addressed them again; but they kept shouting, 'Crucify, crucify him!' A third time he said to them, 'Why, what evil has he done? I have found in him no ground for the sentence of death; I will therefore have him flogged and then release him.' But they kept urgently demanding with loud shouts that he should be crucified; and their voices prevailed. So Pilate gave his verdict that their demand should be granted. He released the man they asked for, the one who had been put in prison for insurrection and murder, and he handed Jesus over as they wished.
LUKE 23:18–25

If you have time today, read the whole account of Jesus' trial and death in Luke 23, from the beginning down to verse 49. All the way through these harrowing events, there are little echoes, little hints, little images of the big truths that are taking place from a heavenly point of view. Read it and see what stands out to you in your memory. Perhaps it's the image of Jesus, silent before Herod as a lamb to the slaughter, a sheep before the shearers (Isaiah 53:7). Perhaps it's the detail, so easy to miss, that Herod and Pilate stopped being enemies and started to be friends from that day (v. 12), the reconciling work of Jesus taking place even as he is condemned to death. Perhaps it's the two criminals on the crosses next to Jesus, one mocking him and the other being welcomed into paradise with him. Or perhaps it is this part, about Barabbas.

Pilate could find no fault in Jesus. Barabbas, on the other hand, was not innocent; he had done the deed. He was already condemned, already imprisoned. Significantly, though, he had done exactly what the crowds on Palm Sunday had hoped Jesus would do: he had probably led, or at least taken part in, some sort of rebellion against Roman rule. The murder he was accused of was probably that of one or more Romans, since it was for these sorts of crimes that the Romans crucified the people whose countries they occupied. He was guilty, but for the people cheering for his release, he was guilty of all the right things. There was a reason they chose him over Jesus.

He even had the same name: in Matthew's gospel he is Jesus Barabbas. It would have been a fairly popular name. The Jesus part, the name that the angel Gabriel told to Mary, means 'rescuer'. (It has the same root as Joshua from the Old Testament.) Barabbas just means 'son of the father'. The rescuer, son of the father? Jesus and Barabbas are easily confused. But one Jesus is the son of a human father, the son of Adam; the other is the son of a heavenly Father, the Son of God.

The crowd choose Barabbas because they want a rescuer from their troubles, a champion who is ready to act passionately on their behalf. In choosing Barabbas over Jesus, that is exactly what they get, but they don't know it because they do not see the bigger picture. Barabbas, on the other hand, might have an inkling. As soon as the other Jesus is chosen for death, he goes free, like the other goat on the day of atonement: one for the Lord and one for the wilderness. He receives freedom and a champion who is ready to die on his behalf. He is the first to experience the rescue that is taking place for all humankind.

If we are honest with ourselves, we choose Barabbas all the time. He is what we opt for when we think that we can have any part in our own rescue. When we list the things we've done well as a defence mechanism against criticism; when we call ourselves good people in comparison to others whom we judge as bad; when we come to God with excuses instead of repentance; and when we look for the human solution to a problem first, we choose Barabbas. The Adam in us always will. Yet every time we do, we unknowingly make another choice: we send Jesus Christ, the innocent one, to a death which will rescue us and set us free, so that instead of being children of Adam, we will become children of the same heavenly Father.

A question

What kinds of problems are you least likely to pray about? Why do you think that is?

A prayer

Lord, whenever I am struggling, remind me to look to you, to call on you, to choose you. Thank you for being ready to listen, to help and to save. Amen

Holy Saturday

Another person's tomb

When it was evening, there came a rich man from Arimathea, named Joseph, who was also a disciple of Jesus. He went to Pilate and asked for the body of Jesus; then Pilate ordered it to be given to him. So Joseph took the body and wrapped it in a clean linen cloth and laid it in his own new tomb, which he had hewn in the rock. He then rolled a great stone to the door of the tomb and went away.

MATTHEW 27:57–60

It's a bit of a strange hobby, I suppose, but when I visit churches I love to spend time reading the gravestones and memorials. Some of them are like flash fiction: tiny stories of love and loss. Some are unbearably sad, others whimsical or inspiring. One of my favourites is in St Andrew's Anglican Church in Pau, France, and it reads: 'God gave her his gift of sympathy for those in sorrow and distress, and so she was beloved.' It makes me wish I had known Nancy Wadsworth Rogers, who died in 1919.

The church in our village here has a memorial to one Zachariah Howe, who died in 1921 and was 'a ringer and singer of this church for 62 years'. I think it's especially touching that he is commemorated in the choir stalls where he served for so long, and that the words of the memorial chime and rhyme as he did. Another of my favourite inscriptions is the very metaphorical one in St Mary's Church, Bury St Edmunds, which is specific to the trade of the person it remembers: Peter Gedge, the printer of Bury's first newspaper, who 'like a worn out Type' is 'returned to the Founder, in hopes of being recast in a better and more perfect Mould'.

Tombs and memorials of the ancient world are no different; often, they hold invaluable information for archaeologists and historians, because the people remembered in them wanted to immortalise themselves by giving every detail of their achievements and generous works. A tomb is a very personal thing. I wonder how much thought Joseph of Arimathea had given to his final resting place. He had hewn a place for himself in a rock; I wonder how he chose the location? Was it on his own land, near his family home? Was there a beautiful view?

Yet Joseph gave up this final resting place of his to Jesus. A secret disciple, and one with plenty of money, he was probably the only person who could have managed to get Jesus' body from Pilate as well as having somewhere to place him safely before the sabbath. Unlike the twelve disciples, who would not have been trusted by the Romans, Joseph of Arimathea was not publicly associated with Jesus; he had kept his interest in him quiet. So Jesus was hastily wrapped in graveclothes and laid in the tomb of a man he had possibly never met.

Once again, we have a fleeting image here of a greater truth. Just as Jesus replaced Barabbas and let him go free, reminding us of what his death did for everyone, so his body was placed in someone else's tomb. Christ died for all. His body lay in your tomb, and in mine; and because of his death and resurrection, all those tombs will one day be opened.

Joseph sealed the tomb with a great stone and then went away. He left the two Marys watching the tomb, and the Roman guards then came to make it secure. But the picture of Joseph closing his own tomb and walking away from it reminds me of Job's image of sin, sealed up and covered over. Jesus has taken sin and death, sealed it up and covered it over in the grave that would have been our own, so that we can walk away, free and alive.

Death has such a finality about it. The soil covering a grave, or the moment the coffin disappears behind the curtain in the crematorium, is the hardest part of a funeral service because it feels like the end of that person we loved. But the sealing of Jesus' tomb was not the end of Jesus; it was the end of the finality of death. Death itself was sealed away, never to return, never to carry the same weight and power. With this image today, and in our celebrations tomorrow, we carry the constant hope that death will never again have the last word.

A question

How does Jesus' death change the way you think about your own death?

A prayer

Lord, Joseph walked away from the tomb that should have been his. Because of your death, I can walk away from the death that should have been mine. Thank you for putting an end to the finality of death. Amen

Easter Sunday

Alleluia!

After the sabbath, as the first day of the week was dawning, Mary Magdalene and the other Mary went to see the tomb. And suddenly there was a great earthquake; for an angel of the Lord, descending from heaven, came and rolled back the stone and sat on it. His appearance was like lightning, and his clothing white as snow. For fear of him the guards shook and became like dead men. But the angel said to the women, 'Do not be afraid; I know that you are looking for Jesus who was crucified. He is not here; for he has been raised, as he said. Come, see the place where he lay. Then go quickly and tell his disciples, "He has been raised from the dead, and indeed he is going ahead of you to Galilee; there you will see him." This is my message for you.' So they left the tomb quickly with fear and great joy, and ran to tell his disciples. Suddenly Jesus met them and said, 'Greetings!' And they came to him, took hold of his feet, and worshipped him. Then Jesus said to them, 'Do not be afraid; go and tell my brothers to go to Galilee; there they will see me.'

MATTHEW 28:1–10

Happy Easter! Christ is risen – he is risen indeed, alleluia!

The hymn 'This joyful Eastertide', which I am sure I shall have sung this morning, puts it best. Paraphrasing Paul in 1 Corinthians 15:14, George Ratcliffe Woodward (1848–1934) wrote:

Had Christ, who once was slain,
not burst his three-day prison,
our faith had been in vain.

Jesus' resurrection is the joyful moment in which the work is complete: death is defeated, sin is buried and the door to everlasting life has been left open forever. It is the start of the new creation, the new life in which the direction of everything is towards God and towards peace.

Today, we can gather up all the images of grace that we have encountered in this book and know that each of them holds an eternal truth about what Christ has done for his beloved world, and for us.

Our God delivers us from death and distance,
twin certainties, of Eve and Adam born;
instead we have eternal life and closeness
all walls collapsed, the temple curtain torn:
for sin has been rolled sideways like a tombstone,
cleaned up, sealed tight, and cast into the sea,
and earth and heaven are once again made one,
and we are free.

A hero fought the giant in my armour,
on my behalf he conquered death with death.
The judge pronounced the verdict and the sentence
and paid the punishment, all in one breath:
for God has drawn a cross from earth to heaven,
from east to west, to call the world to see
that he has reconciled all things together,
and we are free.

Then purify me, Lord, although it pains me:
burn off my dross and dirt without a trace
so you will be reflected in me plainly,
and I will see you clearly face to face.
Great Father, may I leave my sins behind me.
Create a clean heart, write your truth in me,
for you joined heaven and earth to come and find me,
and set me free.

A suggestion

The fasting time of Lent has finished, but now we start the 50-day long feast of Easter, up until Pentecost. Easter is a time of celebration, an opportunity to remember our gratitude for the death and resurrection of Jesus every day, and a season in which to start living the new life that Easter offers us.

Which images of grace will you recall and carry into the days ahead? Have you encountered any new ways of understanding the difference that Christ's death and resurrection makes to you and to the world? I invite you, for every week of the Easter season, perhaps every Sunday, to choose one of the images from this book and interact with it in a grateful way that suits you. This could be going back to the text in the Bible and reading it prayerfully, writing your own prayer or poem of thanks, journalling, drawing or painting your own interpretation of the image, or anything else you can think of.

May your Easter be full of the blessings of God's grace.

Acknowledgements

Writing a book is like running a marathon, and it can't be done without the support and expertise of many others: I would like to take this opportunity to thank them.

First, there are the many cheerers and encouragers, in particular my husband and children, and more widely the wonderful Association of Christian Writers, where I have found so much support over the years.

Then there are the ones holding the signposts and handing out water, who have the expertise and equipment to keep the runner going. A special thank you goes to my sister Cecily, who has been prepared at all times of the day or night to drop whatever she's doing, look up a passage in Greek and talk through the vocabulary with me. Thanks to my parents, too, who gave the book an extra proofread.

Are marathons ever run in teams? My metaphor may have run its course, but I am blessed to be part of a writing trio. In our weekly calls, Tanya Marlow, Amy Boucher Pye and I share everything from triumphs to setbacks, from big new ideas to end-of-project fine tuning. So much that appears in my writing started life in discussion with them. Particular thanks for this book has to go to Tanya, who lovingly coached me through the last week of writing while I had Covid, and more or less carried me over the finish line.

And thanks, of course, to the wonderful team at BRF for their hard work in the editing and design of this book.

New Daylight offers four months of daily Bible reading and reflection for everybody who wants to go deeper with God. It is ideal for those looking for a fresh approach to regular Bible study, and offers a talented team of contributors who present a Bible passage (text included), helpful comment and a prayer or thought for the day ahead. *New Daylight* is edited by Gordon Giles and is published three times a year in January, May and September. Available in regular and deluxe editions with large print, as a daily email and as an app for Android, iPhone and iPad.

New Daylight
Sustaining your daily journey with the Bible
£4.85 per issue, or subscriptions available both for print and app

brfonline.org.uk